
D0481022

- Please return to any Bournemouth Library by the due date.

- Renewals can be made in any Bournemouth Library, by telephone, email, or online via the website.

WESTBOURNE LIBRARY
ALUM CHINE ROAD
BOURNEMOUTH BH4 8DX

BOURNEMOUTH LIBRARIES

630027097 Y

The Family Lawyer's Guide to Separation and Divorce

How to get what you both want

LAURA NASER

Vermilion
LONDON

1 3 5 7 9 10 8 6 4 2

Published in 2019 by Vermilion an imprint of Ebury Publishing,

20 Vauxhall Bridge Road,
London SW1V 2SA

Vermilion is part of the Penguin Random House group of companies
whose addresses can be found at global.penguinrandomhouse.com

Penguin
Random House
UK

Copyright © Laura Naser 2019

Laura Naser has asserted her right to be identified as the author of this
Work in accordance with the Copyright, Designs and Patents Act 1988

First published by Vermilion in 2019

www.penguin.co.uk

A CIP catalogue record for this book is available from the British Library

ISBN 9781785042263

Typeset in 10.75/14.5pt Sabon LT Std
by Integra Software Services Pvt. Ltd, Pondicherry.

Printed and bound in Great Britain by Clays Ltd, Elcograf S.p.A.

Penguin Random House is committed to a sustainable
future for our business, our readers and our planet.
This book is made from Forest Stewardship Council®
certified paper.

Contents

Acknowledgements

I HAVE WANTED TO be a lawyer, and specifically a family lawyer, since the age of 12. My parents and any adult I would tell always seemed to think it impressive and this seemed to keep the idea alive. I didn't know any lawyers: my father grew up on a farm and is an engineer, and my mother was our full-time carer and a medical secretary. My only exposure to the law was from watching TV programmes about court cases, and the occasional careers fair. At secondary school, when it came to obtaining a placement for a week's work experience, I elected for a placement in law. I was told that there was only one place and it had gone to a boy in my class because the teacher thought he was more likely to become a lawyer. This bothered me, and still does today. And so to my first acknowledgement. To the teacher who didn't think I was likely to become a lawyer. You gave me my first experience of needing a thick skin, from which I grew my 'can-do' attitude and determination to pursue law as a career, for which I am thankful.

My parents, Carol and John Whitehouse, my brother, Paul, and my wider family have been my constant support, without which I would most definitely not have got to where I am today. I had just enough freedom to experience while also the stability and comfort to just be. My big brother has kept me on my toes and given me my inherent competitiveness which endures today. My family's encouragement has continued into my adult life and the support I have received to enable me to put pen to paper and actually write a book has been invaluable – thank you.

Dawn Alston, my auntie, was devastatingly and rapidly taken from us at the young age of 47 due to cancer. She arranged for me to have my first work experience in law at the magistrates' court where she sat as a Justice of the Peace. She was passionate, fiery and fierce in her determination, and despite her own busy life and two young children she made time to talk to me about law and pulled what strings she could to give me my first exposure to it. I have you and your encouraging words with me at all times.

My husband has been my personal cheerleader and sense-checker since we met at law school many years ago. His personal striving and achievements set the bar incredibly high and, no matter how competitive I am, I have never been able to exactly compete. But it is that striving to compete, his constant never-wavering encouragement, love and understanding of my passion for what I do that has allowed me to do this. He's been my 'yes man', telling me to reach higher and is always on my shoulder telling me I can do it. It's been a struggle for us both to balance family life, prioritise our children, have our careers and fit in me writing this book. Thank you for it all my darling.

To those in my professional life who have given me platforms upon which I had no idea I could stand, thank you. As a trainee I thought my path was set but I was never fine with where that trajectory was heading. I met June Venters QC, the first female solicitor to become a Queen's Counsel, and she gave me a job as a newly qualified solicitor in her firm. If I thought I was working long hours, I knew she was working more. She showed me what it means to go above and beyond and do it because of a passion and love for family law. I was thrown in at the deep end and the deep end was also on fire. This was my first baptism of fire and I loved it, and I will be forever grateful to June.

Next, to Jane Mitchell and Ruth James of (as it was then) Manches LLP, now Penningtons Manches Cooper LLP. The firm is highly ranked, multidisciplinary and big compared to the boutique practice where I had started to cut my teeth. I had, and still have to this day, imposter syndrome. Jane Mitchell interviewed me and I told her I wanted to be nurtured. She and Ruth did just that and they showed me a world of complex high-end disputes that I had never before experienced. They not only nurtured my professional career, but they nurtured me when, just three months after starting my Associate role with them, I was told I had bowel cancer. The support from them, the wider team and the firm was incredible. For taking a chance, putting on the reins, empowering and nourishing which continues today, thank you.

Years later after having my first child I moved office within the firm to work with Veronica Gilmour to support her in building up a new family team in Guildford. She got me with all my post-maternity leave wobbliness and newness of being a working mum. She has been a professional and personal champion of mine, challenging, guiding and encouraging me. To Veronica, and the rest of the team, thank you.

My friends and others in the profession with whom I have had the pleasure of working alongside and knowing – you are all owed acknowledgement and thanks. My friends near and far are my vital network and grounding who have kept me going, helped me out and championed me in my personal and professional life. Thank you all!

To Jenny Scott of Mothers Meetings for saying yes when I introduced myself and told her we needed to host a family law event together. You have inspired me, allowed me to do things out of my comfort zone and said yes when I wasn't sure myself what exactly it was I was proposing. This same acknowledgement goes to Sam Jackson, my commissioning editor, who approached me about writing this book. This is all possible because of you – thank you. And to Julia Kellaway, for editing me and making sense of it all, thank you!

To my children, who changed me and made me. You have put up with Mummy disappearing off to write, and my daughter now role-plays 'I'm going to write my book' which is something she would never have ordinarily been exposed to from two lawyer parents. Being a working parent is hard, but you've made it as easy on me as you know how, and you make life a joy. Thanks for being your crazy, cute and loving selves. 'We choose to go to the moon.'

Introduction

ECIDING WHETHER TO separate from your partner is one of the biggest decisions you can make – and it's an incredibly emotional one too. I am a family lawyer and clients come to see me when they have separated or are thinking about separating from their partner and need some guidance on how to make co-parenting work, how to separate their worldly goods or how to legally separate. Sometimes clients simply need a nudge in the right direction on what to do next. It is my hope that this book will guide you as if you were in a meeting with me. I will explain the key issues that arise after the breakdown of a relationship, such as concerns about your children, financial worries and how to communicate with each other during this difficult and emotional time. I will also offer essential tips and guidance on how best to proceed and manage your ongoing relationship with your ex-partner, ideally keeping things as amicable as possible and getting through the process efficiently and with minimal upset.

People often worry that taking legal advice early on will somehow cause everything to snowball and will put them on an acrimonious route to separation or divorce. However, in my experience, this is simply not the case. Instead, informing yourself as early as possible will give you the confidence and knowledge to move forward, whether that be to reconcile with your partner or to separate. It's essential that you know what all your options are in order to decide what is best for you and your family.

How to Use This Book

It is important to understand that all family law issues run in parallel with each other. However, as they are not automatically tied together in court proceedings, I have separated out the key topics into individual chapters. In the eyes of the law, the divorce or dissolution process simply formally ends a marriage or civil partnership. There are additional procedures for sorting out issues related to finances and children. For example, the founding issue is the breakdown of your relationship and, if required, the legal termination of that relationship. If you and your partner have children together, the arrangements for them will be another issue that needs to be resolved. However, if you make an application for a divorce, the court will not automatically consider the arrangements for your children – the court trusts that you, as parents, will be able to agree those arrangements yourselves or, if you can't, you will need to make an application to the court about that separately. The same applies to your financial matters. Whether or not you are married, your financial separation and ongoing financial responsibilities to each other will be a separate issue to be resolved. There are obvious crossovers from one issue to another, but it's better to think of them as 'running in parallel' and not intermingled, and that is why they are distinctly separated out in this book. There are various ways in which you can resolve each dispute. For example, you will need to apply to court for a divorce, but if you can agree the arrangements for your children between you, you will not need to apply to the court about that issue as well.

This book will provide you with practical, honest guidance without the fear that matters will somehow escalate if you seek external advice. It's a cost-effective way to be educated by and exposed to an experienced family lawyer and gain practical advice and tips on the best way to move forward. It is my hope that this book will empower you while giving you the time and space to consider matters at your own pace.

KNOW YOUR RIGHTS

This book references the laws of England and Wales on the assumption that you are sufficiently attached to that jurisdiction for the laws to apply to you. If you or your ex-partner is international then it can be a complex issue to determine which country's laws apply to your dispute, and you might need the advice of a lawyer in more than one country to determine that for you (see page 56 for more on this).

The law treats spouses differently to cohabitees. You are a spouse if:

- You and your partner entered into a legal marriage or civil partnership anywhere in the world. (If you are not sure whether your marriage or partnership would be recognised as legal in this country, it's best to take the advice of a lawyer.)

- You entered a legal marriage or civil partnership and have separated already (even if it was years ago) but haven't done anything about formalising your separation.

You are a cohabitee if:

- You live with your partner and have not married (legally).
- You used to live with your partner and separated already (and never married each other or entered a civil partnership).

Just to dispel a myth, there is no such thing as a common-law spouse. Many clients ask me about this, usually when they have been living with their partner for years and, as far as they see it, are married in all but name. I've seen this come up as an option when electing relationship status for things such as car insurance, but in England and Wales it does not exist. The law only treats those who have entered into a legal marriage or civil partnership as a spouse/civil partner, so if you haven't done that you are or were a cohabitee.

PART I

FIRST THINGS FIRST

CHAPTER 1

Finding Support

I T MAY BE that your relationship hasn't been quite the same for some time now. Perhaps you and your partner have slowly drifted apart from each other without a 'trigger' event, such as an affair coming to light or a blowout argument. Consistent and deep changes in your relationship that you feel cannot be reversed, such as a move from affectionate to platonic or going from sharing your lives to simply coexisting, might signal to you that your relationship status has changed for good. Or it may be that you've discovered that your partner has been having an affair and now you're not sure what to do. Whatever led to you picking up this book, it's not for me or anyone else to tell you what you should do or how you should be feeling. There's no right or wrong answer to whether you should try to stay together or go your separate ways. The best thing you can do is to take control of what you can, empower yourself with knowledge and manage your own feelings and actions. It is also important to think about those things that are outside your control, such as your partner's actions or your children's wishes. While you cannot control another person, you can control how their thoughts and actions make you feel and how you react to them. Reading this book is a step in the right direction, and there are several other ways of getting additional help and support.

Relationship Counselling and Therapy

The very mention of the words 'counselling' or 'therapy' can make some people immediately recoil and, if it's not for you, that's fine. However, for those of you who aren't sure or would like to consider it but don't know where to start, I suggest that you look up Relate – 'the relationship people'. Relate is a charity offering relationship support nationwide, so it's likely that you will be able to find a service near you. Even just looking at its website is a useful tool and a good place to start (www.relate.org.uk). Alternative support services can also be found via the British Association for Counselling and Psychotherapy (BACP) or you may have a friend or family member who has been through a similar situation and can make a personal recommendation to you.

It may be that you want to go to counselling on your own to help you to understand why your relationship has changed and how to make improvements before you feel it is beyond repair. Or you may wish to understand why your relationship has broken down and to obtain some tools on how to cope. Alternatively, you might be interested in attending counselling together with your partner or ex-partner to work on your relationship. The environment of counselling is set to provide you with a neutral and safe environment for both of you to feel comfortable enough to talk openly and discuss your issues together. Couples counselling could be the key to your reconciliation or it could enable a better, more amicable, separation. If you are able to separate and retain at least a civil relationship, that can only be a good thing. In my experience, it can be difficult to get both partners to be open to attending counselling sessions, but I strongly feel that it's worth a try. If you know from the outset that your partner is not the couples counselling type, then don't rule out going on your own.

It's worth bearing in mind that counsellors will not be able to give you advice on what will happen if you choose to separate – that's the job of a family lawyer. Counselling is instead an additional support service. I have seen many cases where the emotion of the split impacts negatively upon the separation, the arrangements for the children and the financial settlement. When emotions take over, couples often don't feel so willing to negotiate and settle their issues. I've recommended couples counselling for those who aren't sure what they want, to see if it can assist with a reconciliation, and also to those after the separation and while the divorce is proceeding in the hope that it will give the spouses some clarity on what happened, why their relationship broke down, and how they can communicate and feel better towards each other going forward. I'm not saying counselling works for everyone, but it might be worth a try.

Family and Friends

Your friends and family may be a brilliant support network, but I say 'may be' for a number of reasons. Some people are so early in the process of considering separation that they don't want anyone else to know about their thoughts, worried that airing their concerns will only escalate the situation. Another issue may be that there is a conflict of interests, for example your best friend's partner might be great mates with your partner, and there is therefore a risk that what you have discussed privately could get back to your partner. If you would rather not speak to your family and friends about your thoughts at this time, please don't discount the value in just meeting for a drink and talking about other topics. The social distraction may be all the support you need right now.

Parents are also potentially tricky confidants. Presumably, they are on your team and want the best for you, but that could mean that if you say anything negative about your partner, the mud will stick and it may make their ongoing relationship with your partner awkward, especially if you decide to reconcile. Alternatively, your partner may be just as much a son/daughter to your parents as you are, and therefore they may not be very supportive of you if you are the one who wants to separate.

The 'pub divorce lawyer' is a danger to look out for. A relative or friend may have been through an acrimonious split, which then taints the advice they give to you. Every family and every separation is different, so proceed with caution when such friends (who, of course, are only trying to help) give you advice as their experiences are unlikely to be relevant to you. Equally, the 'search engine lawyer' comes with hundreds of red flags. Though there are lots of brilliant online resources that might give you a bit of knowledge to make you feel better about how to move forward, the nature of the Internet is international and filled with different opinions. It's therefore important to ensure that the resources you are using are relevant – reading articles about divorce will not assist you if it turns out they relate to the laws of an American state for example. Bear in mind that it is not always obvious which country online articles relate to. If your source is an online community for discussion then the caution of the pub divorce lawyer applies!

You might feel like you need some space to reflect, think about what you want and gain some perspective, away from your shared home. Taking a short break away and gaining some distance can be very useful for your mind and soul. However, it's important to communicate the purpose and length of your trip with your partner to gain their support and enable an easy return. Leaving your shared home, even temporarily, may have its advantages but be warned that it might also come with disadvantages if your partner decides to take the opportunity to (wrongly) do something like move your belongings out or change the locks.

Medical Help

There may be more complex issues causing the breakdown in your relationship, such as drink or substance misuse, gambling addiction or health issues, including physical or mental health. There is all sorts of professional help available for these situations and it's probably better to focus on what help can be put into place for any issues such as this as a priority, unless your separation is for your own or your children's well-being and/or safety. A good place for you to start is likely to be with your GP, even if it's your partner with the problem. For example, if your partner has a drinking problem and it is impacting on your relationship to the extent that you are considering a separation, speaking to your GP may help you to work out how to cope with the situation. Your GP may also be able to point you in the right direction to get your partner some assistance. Whatever the issue, have a think about what services might help; these may include addiction services, anger management courses, parenting classes or therapy.

If your situation is more serious and you feel that you and/ or your children are in immediate danger of harm – whether that be physical or emotional – then you really need to seek assistance from the police, and if you require protective orders to be put in place, you will need to speak to a family lawyer. If you feel at risk you should not hesitate to obtain assistance, and quickly.

Part of being a family lawyer is not just advising my clients on the law, but also being practical in my advice. Thinking practically can be hard when you are the one going through the separation and feeling the emotion of it, which is why having a lawyer early on can be a real advantage, giving you access to someone who can help you think through your options with clarity. I want to help to make your separation work in your unique circumstances, which means that, as much as possible, it should make sense for you, meet your children's needs and stay within your financial means, while also keeping one eye on what will work for you emotionally.

It is my hope that this book will lead you through your options at your own pace, be a point of reference and give you some confidence to move forward, not only within the boundaries of what the law offers you, but also with some ideas on how to be creative to make your next steps work for you.

PART II

THE ESSENTIAL
SEPARATION TOOLKIT

CHAPTER 2

Options for Separation

I F SEPARATION IS on the cards, whether that be your choice or a decision made by your partner (it might be that you don't want to separate but your partner has chosen it), then your head is probably spinning right now. Clarity is the best starting point. You have a few options available to you, again without risk of the snowball factor.

Separation can mean a few things and relates to you whether you are married, in a civil partnership or in an unmarried relationship. It could be that you just want to separate to give yourself some space to think and reflect. This is known as a 'temporary separation' and it can give both you and your partner the comfort of knowing that the door to reconciliation remains open, but for now you are having some time apart. Alternatively, you may have already made the decision that your relationship has ended and reconciliation is not an option. Your separation is therefore permanent. It's now a matter of deciding how to unravel that separation, which includes sorting out your physical separation, any legalities of that separation (such as divorce), how your children will spend their time between you and your financial separation.

Being separated, whether temporarily or permanently, does not mean that you must be physically separated. It is very common for couples to separate but continue to live under the same roof. There are two main reasons for this. The first is because they can't immediately afford two homes, so one person may move into the spare room or share a room with a child as a temporary measure until their financial separation is finalised. The second reason is because of the children. Couples recognise the importance of a stable home life and, in the absence of deciding about the permanency of their separation or having sorted out their financial separation, they think it is best to stay in the same home to maintain a stable home life for their children, who may or may not be aware of their parents' separation.

When considering separating from your partner, it is worth bearing in mind that there are different factors that are likely to persuade you in deciding the extent of your separation. For those who are unmarried, your options are either a temporary or permanent separation. For those who are married, you have those same two options, and also legal means of separation, such as a divorce which formally ends your marriage. The legal ending of a marriage by divorce may be ruled out by some due to a variety of concerns, such as:

- Religion
- Pressure from family and friends
- Fear of the unknown
- Worry about the cost and financial separation
- A preference to raise children in a two-parent household

Divorce may not form part of your belief system, for social or religious reasons, and you could instead consider either an informal separation or a legal separation. Or, for those who are close to retirement, your pension may be a significant asset of the marriage and you might find it is financially better for you not to divorce due to how your pension scheme works. In those scenarios, legal separation (which is different to a divorce) or an informal separation may be more suited to you. However, for the majority of separating married couples who have decided that their relationship with their partner is over, divorce is the most used method of ending their marriage. If your relationship has broken down to the extent that reconciliation is not a possibility, then staying together for any of the above reasons is unlikely to be a healthy decision and, as you work through the book, I hope you'll see that there are ways to relieve and address all of these concerns.

Temporary Separation

Temporary separation is an option for those who are just not sure what they want to do. There is no timescale on a 'temporary' separation – you can just take it day by day – but sometimes people find it helpful to have a 'review' date, which will depend on why you want to temporarily separate. Often a period of a matter of weeks is time enough for reflection, but if there are significant issues to be worked on in the intervening period, three to six months may be a more realistic time frame for a review. The benefit of a temporary separation is that it gives you time to work on yourself and on your relationship if you think you might want to reconcile. The practicalities of this come down to your family's financial situation. If you or your partner moves into the spare room, is that enough space for you to have some time to think? You'll still be sharing the rest of the house and the facilities, and will have to live around each other every day. That might be fine if you're still getting along, but not so good if there's any animosity. This is where a lawyer's practical advice can assist you in deciding what you want to do.

If you don't want your children to be aware that you are temporarily separated, staying under the same roof might be a good way of maintaining a stable home life for them, but only if you and your partner are both able to be civil and make it work. If you don't have a spare room, this option is trickier. You can try setting up a spare bed in a child's room and sharing with them, or changing an office or dining room into a temporary bedroom, but this probably won't be suitable for very long and, depending on the age of your children, it is likely to attract questions from them about the reason behind the new sleeping arrangements.

Another option is to stay with family or friends – 'sofa-surfing' – but this tends to be much more time-limited as you don't want to outstay your welcome. This can also trigger negative emotions towards the partner that remains in the house, having it 'easier' by not having to rely on the generosity of others and continuing to enjoy the comfort of their own home. This option also means that you will have to bite the bullet and 'go public', to some extent, about your relationship problems.

If finances allow, you could consider moving to a hotel or renting a home on a short-term rental agreement. The obvious financial concerns apply here, in addition to the potential for conflicting emotions about having to be the one to 'move out', and concerns about the impact it may have on your children.

In my experience, moving out of the family home, particularly so if it is initially intended to only be on a temporary basis, is not always advisable. Although you might both agree now that it's just temporary, what happens if the result of your temporary separation is that you want to reconcile and move back but your spouse doesn't agree? It's often much harder for you to move back into the family home once you're out, even if you are one of the legal owners. As a spouse or co-owner, you have legal rights to occupy the marital home but the reality is that it will be an uphill struggle to do so if your partner who remains living there does not want you to move back in.

If you think a temporary separation is right for you, it's important to think about these practical issues:

- Do you want to stay under the same roof or be separate?
- Which one of you will be the one to move out (of the bedroom or home)?
- Where will you both sleep and for how long could this be manageable?
- What boundaries can you put in place if you continue to share your home together, albeit separated? Will you continue to cook for each other and even eat together?
- How will you share the house chores, such as laundry and cleaning? It may be that part of the cause of your disputes is due to these kinds of issues building up, so is it realistic for you to remain living together with these ongoing concerns?
- If you or your partner moves out to a hotel or short-term rental, is that affordable and for how long will it be affordable? From what, or whose, resources will it be funded?
- If one of you moves out, what arrangements can you put in place for your children to spend time with each

of you? You'll also need to think about how and when you explain the changes to them.

- What happens if you do not reconcile?
- What will each of you be doing during the separation period to help resolve your issues, with a view to reconciliation or in deciding how to separate? For example, will you go to counselling or see a family lawyer or financial advisor?

If you decide to reconcile

If after a temporary separation you decide to reconcile, you should consider whether to take or continue with any external support services such as counselling or therapy either individually or together. The foundations of your relationship are likely to have been rocked by your temporary separation so it is worth giving them some attention as a preventative step going forward.

From a legal perspective, you might feel more secure and comfortable with your reconciliation by entering into either a cohabitation agreement or nuptial agreement with your partner. These are legal contracts between you which set out what you agree should happen if your relationship breaks down again, either temporarily or, more commonly, permanently. They are a great idea for those whose temporary separation was caused by financial issues, as they focus on the financial consequences of your future separation. A cohabitation agreement is used for unmarried couples, a prenuptial agreement is used for engaged couples ahead of a wedding and a postnuptial agreement can be made at any time after a wedding by a married couple. These agreements act as a contract between you so you go back into your relationship knowing that if you were to separate again you know what you would separate with. For those who enter into nuptial agreements, it's worth bearing in mind that they are not automatically binding on a later divorce, but if entered into properly and with legal advice on both sides, they are considered very persuasive and likely to be upheld by a judge.

If you decide to go your separate ways

If you conclude that your relationship has come to an end and you do not want to reconcile, you will need to communicate this to your partner. This decision is rarely one mutually made at the same time. One partner tends to have come to this conclusion ahead of the other and therefore has longer to come to terms with it, and think ahead to practical arrangements about how it might work with respect to your children and financially.

Tone, reason and explanation will be key to successfully communicating your decision to your partner. Think carefully about timing, where you will have the talk and the message you want to put across. Being considerate and amicable at this early stage will help you to set the tone going forward, which is particularly important if you have children together. If you are ahead of your partner in coming to this conclusion about your relationship then, understandably, they are likely to be shocked and not immediately in a position to talk about the detail of how your separation will work. You should not tell your partner that you want to end your relationship and at the same time expect to discuss one of you leaving your shared home, the arrangements for how you will each spend time with your children, and how your finances should be split.

Emotions will be running high which means reason and understanding will suffer. If you approach this situation from a place of kindness, at least as much as possible depending on your reason for separation, it will increase your chances of your separation being civil. Try to give each other time and space in between discussions so that you can collaboratively work through the logistics of your separation and don't put each other under any unnecessary or unreasonable pressure. For example, saying 'I'm leaving and I'm going to stop paying towards our mortgage or rent and bills' will cause immediate panic and fear. To do so would be unreasonable of you (although, there are the rare occasions where I have seen it necessary, but that should be done with the benefit of legal advice), and it is easy to see how being civil with each other becomes much more difficult. In my opinion there is never a reason to 'declare war' when you decide to separate. Don't be aggressive and unreasonable in your expectations.

Telling your family and friends will be a difficult task. They will have their own emotions and opinions about your separation and it will be necessary for you to manage them to enable you to cope. While there is no doubt that your own family and friends will be coming from a place of concern for you, they may not be privy to all of the information and it is understandable that you would not want to repeat all the detail to others. The more people who know of your separation, the more people who are likely to want to talk about it with you, and give you their opinion. Each situation is different and your willingness to involve others and take opinion is likely to change as you go through your separation, which may last a few months or even years if children's issues become regularly problematic.

Remember that if you have children together, you will have an ongoing relationship with your now ex-partner and your family and friends will need to be supportive. If you don't have children together, you are still likely to have ongoing ties and cross paths again in the future, such as mutual friends inviting you both to the same events. It may not feel like an immediate priority but it's important to manage those around you, with regards to how much information they are given and how widely they share their opinions about your separation. This will take thought and careful communication, but you will probably find that there is a natural filtering of those in your inner circle and anyone on the outside of that inner circle is given less detail and therefore the strength of their opinions and involvement will also be limited.

Permanent Separation

Unmarried couples

If the decision is made that your relationship is over and you will not reconcile, then as an unmarried couple, you can, to some extent 'simply' go your separate ways. If you have children together, then of course you will need to make arrangements for them to continue to spend time with both of you. If you have financial ties, you will also need to unravel those and resolve any financial disputes between you, and it is usually better for that to happen sooner rather than later. This book has sections on both of these issues for you (see Part IV and Chapter 12).

Married couples

If you make the decision that your relationship is over and you are either married or in a civil partnership, you can choose to remain married and simply have a permanent separation. This is not common or usually advisable because as spouses you have rights against and responsibilities towards each other which will continue until you legally end them. To do that, you will need to apply to a court to, most commonly, formally end your marriage with a divorce or your civil partnership with a dissolution. Whichever one applies to you, the process is very similar, so for simplicity I shall refer to both collectively as divorce.

To obtain a divorce you must have been married for at least one year before you make the application to the court. If you have not yet reached your first anniversary then you will either need to wait, consider whether annulment might apply to you (though be warned, it's rare, see page 25) or you could opt for a judicial (also known as a 'legal') separation (see page 26).

Please bear in mind my top tip which is that you should try to be as amicable as possible throughout this process. Your separation is about to become very real and it's not going to make much difference to the divorce process if you go in hard or soft. Try to be as soft as allowable, for your own sake. If the process has already been started by your spouse in a manner which you think is too aggressive or, put simply, just mean, see what can be done to calm the situation down and see if a lighter approach can be assumed. A family lawyer may be needed in this situation to help you to pull it back on to a better track or to take a step to at least protect your position, if need be.

In England and Wales there is only one ground for divorce, which is that your marriage has irretrievably broken down. You don't need to have tried to reconcile first for you to conclude that you want a divorce, but you do have to explain the reason for the breakdown by one of five 'facts', as they are known (see Chapter 3).

Annulment

If you have not yet been married for one year and you do not want to wait until your first anniversary to apply for a divorce, you can consider whether to apply for a decree of nullity. This is not the same as a divorce as it is asking the court to say that your marriage was either void and therefore upon decree of nullity you are treated as never married, or that your marriage was valid but now annulled. This is not an option for the impatient, and strict rules apply as to the circumstances in which a nullity can be sought. These circumstances include:

- the marriage has not been consummated
- it is a bigamous marriage
- no consent was given to the marriage
- at the time of the marriage either spouse was suffering from a mental disorder
- the wife was pregnant by someone else at the time of the marriage
- a spouse has changed gender since the marriage
- either spouse was underage (18 years) or under 16 years without consent of a parent at the time of the marriage

A nullity can be sought immediately after the wedding, and up to three years after the marriage. The court may still make some orders in respect to spousal financial claims, but those financial claims are not as wide as they could be when dealt with alongside a divorce.

Judicial Separation

Judicial, also known as 'legal', separation is a rarity as it is not a divorce or a nullity. With a judicial separation, you remain married and the marriage does not need to have irretrievably broken down. The court effectively relieves you both from your relationship as husband and wife, and you would not be expected to live together anymore. This option is attractive to those who have religious or moral reasons as to why they would not seek a divorce, but who would like to somehow formalise their separation in the eyes of the law. At the time of writing, it must be proved on one of the same five facts as used for a divorce, but the procedure is slightly different. If the intended new Divorce and Judicial Separation bill comes into force as expected in 2020, then it is currently understood that you will not need to prove anything, but simply give a statement stating your wish to be judicially separated to the court. This can be done by either a statement from one spouse or a joint statement from both spouses together. The court can make some financial orders for the spouses, but not to the same extent that they can on divorce.

Your Interim Finances

As part of your discussion about your options for how your separation might work, you will need to discuss finances and how you will be able to afford to separate along with each of your existing financial commitments. You might be financially reliant on each other and must continue to trust each other, which may or may not be easy. For example, if you have a mortgage in your joint names, even if you agree that you will both continue to contribute towards the monthly repayments, what happens if one of you doesn't keep to your word? This has the potential to jeopardise the security of your family home, affect both of your credit ratings and will have consequences on your ability to trust each other (and therefore your amicability) going forward.

Even if you decide to separate but remain living in the same house, you should still talk about money. This could be to make sure that you both commit to maintaining the status quo and continuing to each pay as you have to date. It might be that financial issues have been a cause of your separation, and so agreeing to financial adjustments might be part of your requirements for a reconciliation to be possible.

If one of you is going to move out of the family home, even temporarily, it will be much better to talk about money before that move takes place so that you are both clear on who will pay for what and hopefully avoid any uncertainties further down the line. The key here is to communicate about your own expectations and affordability. It's unlikely to be easy, especially where finances have been a cause for argument between you in the past, but it will be important for both of you to understand exactly who will pay for what, and what will or won't happen with any assets you each have or own together, such as a family car or even the more significant assets such as your home.

If you feel unsure about what your expectations should be, how far your rights extend over each other's assets or what your legal liability is to your soon-to-be-ex-partner, I recommend taking bespoke legal advice at this early stage. Agreeing to something now without the benefit of legal advice could be something you later regret or could simply be unaffordable in the long run. I explain more about the law and financial rights to give you an idea of how the law might apply to you in Part V, but as you will come to understand, the application of the law differs depending on your specific circumstances.

You cannot take legal advice together with your partner or see the same lawyer separately. This is because your legal advisor will tell you how the law applies to you, explain your various options and set out your best- and worst-case scenarios, and this advice might conflict with the advice given to your partner. You do not need to tell your partner that you have taken legal advice, but you might feel that by disclosing it to your partner it gives a bit more validity to your voice. At this stage, you can also use mediation to help you talk about your interim financial arrangements, and I explain what mediation is and how it works on page 81. However, it is important to remember that a mediator cannot legally advise you.

For your immediate financial situation, my advice is to maintain the status quo as much as possible. If the status quo was causing the initial relationship difficulties then try to redress that issue as part of the separation talks, but it is best to do so with the benefit of legal advice as it will be catered to your situation. I would not recommend closing any joint accounts, transferring joint assets or hosting a garage sale full of your ex-partner's belongings. Deal with all of this as part of your overall settlement and don't do anything in haste, anger or revenge. I understand that emotions can run high and it is difficult to control those emotions, particularly so when you feel like your ex-partner is being unreasonable and unkind to you, but doing anything rash is unlikely to assist you in the long run, and will most certainly worsen relations between you.

One knee-jerk reaction is to make a dive for financial paperwork, but it is important to make sure that any paperwork you take is addressed to you solely or jointly with your partner. If you have not been given consent to take the original or a make a copy of a document that is not addressed to you, you cannot take it. You should also not go on the hunt for documents that are not yours. I recommend making a chronological note of what you can remember about each of your financial positions and how they have changed during your relationship, to include significant details, such as who paid for, earned or received what, how much and when.

Remember that if you have accounts in your joint names then you both have equal entitlement to access those accounts and are entitled to half of the funds. You will also have equal responsibility for any liabilities. If you are concerned about your ex-partner suddenly emptying the account or taking it into an overdraft (and you therefore being jointly liable for that debt), you can speak to your bank about your own access and whether they can limit withdrawals or always require joint instructions from you. It might be best to seek a transfer of a joint account, and its balance or a share of the balance, into your sole name so that you can be sure that direct debits can continue to be met. This will require a commitment from your ex-partner to continue to make contributions to the account, unless you are self-sufficient or have agreed it as part of your short-term plans.

Don't forget about savings accounts or joint investments, such as ISAs, premium bonds or shares. These, too, should be maintained as they were prior to your separation, awaiting division as part of your overall financial separation. If one of you needs to access some funds to assist with part of the separation, talk about how that can be afforded and balanced out as part of your later overall settlement. For example, you might agree that some funds will be given to the partner who is to move out to meet a rental deposit and furnishings to cover their immediate housing needs. Depending on affordability, that transfer can be considered as an advance of their share of the final settlement.

It is common for savings to be dipped into or debt to increase when going through a separation because of the extra costs of two homes and, if you choose, obtaining legal advice and other support services. Whichever way you decide to finance yourself throughout this interim period between separation and the final resolution of your issues, be mindful of how your financial decisions will affect the overall joint financial picture. Being unreasonable about your ex-partner accessing joint funds to meet genuine interim needs is likely to be counterproductive and only serve to reduce the overall finances. This ethos is particularly important to bear in mind if you are married, and less so if you are not as the law applies differently to you. Forcing your ex-partner to take out a loan, or a specialist legal fees loan which can attract higher rates of interest or fees, means the money must be repaid from somewhere, and this is usually ultimately from the joint money. I do understand that it might be the only choice to incur debt, but, where you can, try to keep an eye on the bigger picture and be reasonable. Most people tend to panic at the thought of distributing savings at this early stage and want to go into 'lock down' to preserve what you each have for final settlement, so if you are in any way unsure, seek professional advice so that your specific financial situation and circumstances are understood and the law is applied accordingly.

Drawing up a separation agreement

If you want to sort out your financial settlement now and wait for a divorce then your financial agreement should be formally set out in a separation agreement. By recording your agreement formally, it can become contractual between you and gives you both some protection to rely upon the agreement you have reached going forward. The separation agreement would not be binding upon a judge if, at the time of your later divorce, one of you seeks a change to the terms you had earlier agreed, but it would be persuasive and taken into account by a judge, and there would need to be good reason why a judge should not uphold the earlier agreement. With this comes risk, and potential for having to go through the same financial process twice (and incurring the costs of doing so twice over), which is the main reason why proceeding with a divorce at the earlier stage gives you more certainty and cost benefit to move on with your life.

To draw up a separation agreement you will need to go through the same process as for negotiating a final financial settlement (see Chapter 13). If a family lawyer drafts the separation agreement for you it is likely to be more detailed and well-considered than if you draft something between yourselves, thereby increasing the chances of the agreement being upheld at the later date of your divorce.

CHAPTER 3

Divorce or Dissolution of Your Civil Partnership

A s FAR AS the law is concerned, at the time of writing, you must have concluded that your marriage has irretrievably broken down to apply for a divorce (remember that I am including civil partnership and dissolution when I refer to marriage and divorce for ease of explanation). To show this, you are required to explain the reason for the breakdown by one of these five 'facts':

1. Adultery
2. Unreasonable behaviour
3. Two years' separation with consent
4. Five years' separation
5. Desertion

Of those, the most commonly relied upon are one of the first three. Due to the international nature of our media, you may have heard of divorce on the grounds of 'irreconcilable differences'. That's American and not something that can be used in England and Wales.

Unfortunately, currently in England and Wales if you are relying on adultery, unreasonable behaviour or desertion, you must lay blame on your spouse to prove that they have caused the irretrievable breakdown of your marriage. There's been quite a lot in the press recently about changing this to a no-fault divorce, which is available in some other countries. At the time of writing, it's been agreed that our laws will include a no-fault option in the near future, but that's not yet possible if you want to divorce in England and Wales now. The future change will remove the need to explain how your spouse has behaved unreasonably or live separately for a minimum of two years, and instead you will need to give a statement to confirm your marriage has irretrievably broken down. It is also proposed that spouses can jointly apply for a divorce. The timeframe for this being introduced is currently unknown. (See 'Divorce Dissolution and separation Act 2019', page 57 below for more information about these intended changes.)

To start the process based on adultery, unreasonable behaviour or desertion, you are forced by the law to effectively sling a bit of mud at your spouse, which is not then conducive to you being amicable or, probably more importantly, setting the right tone for you to then settle any issues regarding your children and/or finances. You will therefore need to think carefully about what you are going to say, how you are going to say it and how much it will upset your spouse to say that about them and your marriage.

Adultery

To be able to rely on adultery, there must have been sexual intercourse between one spouse and someone of the opposite sex. You cannot rely on adultery if the extramarital intercourse was with someone of the same sex, which is probably not in accordance with most people's thresholds for what constitutes adultery. If you are in a same-sex marriage or civil partnership, your spouse/civil partner must have had sex with someone of the opposite sex for you to use the adultery fact to seek a divorce/dissolution.

Most people would think there are stages of an affair before sexual intercourse which would count as 'cheating', but that's the difference between an affair and adultery. If you found out that your spouse was having a relationship which you thought to be inappropriate because of things that were being said or images being shared, that alone would not be enough to qualify as adultery, but you could use that as an example of your spouse's unreasonable behaviour. Likewise, if you are in a same-sex marriage/civil partnership you could cite your spouse/civil partner's same-sex sexual intercourse as an example of your spouse/civil partner's unreasonable behaviour.

If, after finding out about your spouse's adultery, you try to carry on with your marriage and continue to live together for a period of more than six months as husband and wife, you cannot then later rely on that act of adultery as a ground for divorce. You are seen to have 'forgiven' that act of adultery once that six-month period has passed. The six-month period does not start until the date that you found out about the adultery, and it only starts if you live with each other as 'husband and wife'. For example, say your spouse had a one-night stand in March 2012 but you only found out about it in January 2020. If you choose to continue with your marriage, your six-month period would expire in July 2020. If you try to reconcile for five months but decide the marriage is over, you can still rely on that act of adultery in the divorce petition, if you wish. If after finding out about the adultery you separate but continue to live in the same house, this does not start the six-month time limit as you are not continuing to live as 'husband and wife'.

If you find out that your spouse has committed adultery on more than one occasion, whether it was with the same person each time or not, you will have a period of six months to trial a reconciliation after each time you find out about a new act of adultery. This also means that if you reconciled after disclosure of your spouse's first act of adultery but later find out that your spouse either did it again or had omitted to tell you about another time (even if that was prior to your reconciliation), you can rely on this new knowledge of adultery for divorce. The important date here is the date that you found out about the adultery, not the date the act of adultery happened. You need not prove the date that you found out, unless your divorce application is contested by your spouse. Your own account of how and when you found out is sufficient for an uncontested divorce. For a divorce based on adultery your spouse must admit to it, so usually the date that your spouse admitted their adultery to you is the date replied upon.

Adultery would also apply in the situation where you have separated from your spouse and one or both of you have moved on to form new relationships. If a sexual relationship with a new partner of the opposite sex has started (even a one-night stand), it can be relied upon as an act of adultery for the divorce, even though it occurred post-separation. This might be an attractive option because, although it is legally adultery, it occurred after you had separated so, emotionally, it may not trigger the same feelings as it would if it occurred pre-separation.

I have clients who feel very strongly about basing their divorce petition on their spouse's adultery. Usually, this stems from a wish to record the factual reason for their marriage ending. If it weren't for their partner's adultery, they would still be continuing in their marriage. Often, their feelings of being wronged and wanting to be accurate in the laying of blame can be important to their own ability to move forward. For others, it's a choice: their spouse has committed adultery, but they would rather not document that as the reason in their divorce papers. This is commonly because they believe their spouse will not admit to their adultery, and they want to avoid the downturn in relations it will likely cause if they push the issue.

As part of the divorce process your spouse will be required to admit that they have committed adultery. This does not mean getting them to sign a confession (although this can be useful), but it does mean telling your spouse that you are going to base your divorce petition on their adultery and checking in advance that they will not deny it. Neither you nor they are required to say who they committed adultery with in the divorce petition, and in accepting that they did commit adultery, your spouse is not required to provide any of the details of the adultery. It is simply a 'yes or no' answer on the court form.

If you are the one who has committed adultery you might be feeling a bit nervous about whether to admit to it. There seems to be two repeated concerns from clients when they are the adulterer. The first is that they think they will be penalised for it, whether it be in the divorce or financial settlement, or when it comes to deciding the arrangements for their children. In practice these are both true and untrue. In law, the person who committed adultery is not put in a lesser position. It is not assumed that they should suffer financial loss and, most certainly, children will not be withheld from spending time with that parent because of their act of adultery.

However, how your spouse feels about your adultery can influence any 'penalties'. This relates to your spouse and not the law. While in law there should not be a penalty, your spouse may feel very strongly about your adultery and use those strong feelings in how they deal with you in the divorce process, how they approach your financial settlement and how they feel towards you when planning arrangements for your children. There is no legal grounding for taking this stance so it is unlikely that your spouse will expressly say 'I don't think the children should spend half of the Easter holiday with you because you cheated on me'. However, their self-imposed 'penalties' on you may come dressed up as other issues when perhaps they would not have been if they weren't feeling so upset or angry about your adultery. Likewise, trying to negotiate a financial settlement with an angry spouse is not going to be particularly easy for you.

The second repeated concern is that the adulterer doesn't feel that their adultery alone caused the breakdown of their marriage. My clients who committed adultery often tell me that their marriage was over before they committed adultery and/or that they feel like their spouse's behaviour caused their marriage to fail before the adultery occurred. They then feel that it's unfair to base the divorce on their adultery. I'm not saying here that the adultery should be denied. If there is a suspicion of adultery and lies are told to hide it, then that brings more negativity to an already negative situation. Dishonesty and a lack of integrity are damaging and will further break down what trust was left between you.

For those of you whose spouse has refused to admit that they have committed adultery but you feel strongly that you want to divorce based on their adultery, you need to make a decision as to whether to set out to prove the adultery, which is often difficult, or to opt for the unreasonable behaviour option instead. If your spouse refuses to admit to their adultery, it would mean that the divorce becomes contested. You would then need to produce evidence that your spouse has had sex with someone of the opposite sex, and not many people want to go down this route. Contested divorces are costly and protracted and only serve to worsen relations between you.

If adultery is a potential reason for your divorce, think carefully about whether your spouse is likely to admit to it. If you think they will not want to divorce based on their adultery, I recommend considering a divorce based on your spouse's unreasonable behaviour instead. Clients tend to have good instincts about whether their spouse will be inclined to accept (and therefore admit) to the divorce going ahead based on their adultery, or whether it is likely to do further harm to their already fragile relationship.

This thought process can be the difference between starting off your divorce on the 'rocky but all right' path or the 'doomed for arguments, increased costs and time wasted' path. I've experienced both with my clients, but you don't need me to tell you that one will cause you far more hassle, emotional strain, stress and money than it's worth. That's not to say that you should avoid a divorce reasoned by adultery and it is understandable for the wronged spouse to feel justified in wanting this when it is available and an accurate reflection of the situation. It's just that if you think it's likely to be an inflammatory move, try to avoid it as there are other options and it should not make any legal difference when it comes to your financial separation or your arrangements for your children.

The end goal is a permanent separation from your partner and if switching your reason from adultery to unreasonable behaviour increases your chances of the divorce progressing more smoothly and with fewer arguments and less damage to your relationship, then it is likely to be a wise decision. If you have children together, it is even more important to keep the divorce process and financial separation as amicable as possible. You might have lawyers to help you through this now but once these legal matters are over you will need to co-parent and the lawyers won't be there for you to hide behind or communicate through.

Having said this, if adultery applies and you both agree to proceed with a divorce on this basis then I would say that it can be the most straightforward option. You only need to write two short sentences setting out when you were informed of the adultery, when the adultery happened and that in consequence you believe that your marriage has irretrievably broken down. This clear-cut process means that the divorce has the hope of being amicable and time- and cost-effective.

When using the ground of adultery to seek a divorce there is the option of naming the third party who was involved in the adulterous relationship. Initially you might feel upset enough to want to name that person but it is unlikely to make you feel any better about the situation. Instead it will only increase tension and add more stress. To name that person means they will become part of the divorce proceedings and will need to be sent copies of the divorce documents and engage in the process. It is not something I would advise doing as it is acrimonious, increases the costs of the divorce as there is another person to deal with and means an added layer of complication without much, if any, benefit to you.

Unreasonable behaviour

To prove that your marriage has irretrievably broken down based on your spouse's unreasonable behaviour, you must explain in the divorce application (known as the 'petition', see page 45) that your spouse has behaved in such a way that you cannot reasonably be expected to live with them. You are required to write down examples of your spouse's unreasonable behaviour. Usually four or five very short paragraphs are sufficient, although I have seen some clients who have gone to town and written over ten!

There is a conflict over how 'unreasonable' the behaviour needs to be to sufficiently prove that you can no longer be expected to remain married to your spouse. Most family lawyers will encourage their clients to write anodyne and rather tame examples of their spouse's behaviour, on the basis that you just need to say enough to get the petition approved by a judge, without having to unduly upset your spouse. This advice is given in the hope of getting through the process as amicably as possible. Until recently, this has been the approved method. However, there has been a slight shift from the courts which have effectively said that you need to explain why your spouse's behaviour is so unreasonable that you cannot be expected to live with them any longer. The examples of their behaviour in the petition would therefore need to evidence this to a judge.

In my opinion, the traditional lawyer's approach of prioritising being applicable and anti-inflammatory still applies. Write examples which are not going to trigger an argument, but lay enough blame for your spouse's behaviour to be accepted as unreasonable. In my experience, you and your spouse should agree first on what is going to be said in the divorce petition. If your spouse knows what you are going to say about their unreasonable behaviour before you send the petition to the court, it can be agreed that they will not seek to defend the petition, and therefore there will not be contested proceedings before a judge, and your petition based on your spouse's unreasonable behaviour should be approved. If your spouse does not agree and seeks to contest your examples of their unreasonable behaviour, a judge will need to determine whether they meet the threshold of being so unreasonable you cannot continue to live with your spouse, and are sufficient for the divorce to proceed. If you have sent your spouse a draft of your petition before you send it to the court, you will know at that stage whether your more amicable approach will succeed. If your spouse indicates that they do not accept what you propose to say about them as truthful, and therefore they intend on defending your petition, you can amend your draft examples accordingly and therefore avoid a contested divorce.

What counts as unreasonable behaviour is up to you: what do you find unreasonable about your spouse's behaviour and why? Asking yourself that question will be the answer to you drafting your examples for the divorce petition. There are examples of unreasonable behaviour that society sets for us:

- violence and abuse
- illegal behaviour, such as taking non-prescription drugs
- controlling behaviour, such as limiting your access to money or telling you what you can and cannot do

Then there are the tamer examples, those which have been traditionally preferred by family lawyers as 'more amicable':

- not socialising together, leaving you to feel isolated and lonely
- not supporting and encouraging you in a particular passion or endeavour
- no longer being affectionate and loving towards you
- being unkind and using derogatory remarks about you and/or your family/friends

The behaviour cited must be true and accurate. Hopefully you can see the difference in the levels of inflammation such allegations of unreasonable behaviour are likely to cause.

If you think that your spouse is unlikely to admit to adultery and you have no evidence that adultery has been committed but you feel strongly that an inappropriate relationship with another person has happened, you can include that allegation as an example of your spouse's unreasonable behaviour. Approach this option with a little bit of caution because of the inflammation it is likely to cause between you. Is there something else you could say that is less likely to trigger animosity and therefore hopefully keep you both as amicable as possible in the circumstances? I think this last question is a good standard against which to check each example of unreasonable behaviour that you propose to include.

Two years' separation with consent

If you have lived separately from your spouse for two years then you can divorce based on that minimum length of separation, if your spouse consents to the divorce. Your spouse must give their consent for this ground of two years' separation to be sufficient for a divorce.

The test for separation is whether you live independently of each other, but that does not mean that you have lived in separate homes. A lot of spouses cannot immediately afford to physically separate and so they agree that they will live separately under the same roof. To live separately while still in the same home, you should really live as you would if you were in separate properties. This means preparing meals and eating them separately, doing your own laundry and spending spare time independent of your spouse. The reality, especially when there are children at home, is that there will probably be occasions when you eat together, or your clothes get mixed in the washing machine, or where you both sit in the same room to watch TV. I think that's fine to an extent. The point is that both of you consider your marriage to be over and, as much as possible, you are separated, albeit living under the same roof. It is not a separation where you are also attempting a reconciliation.

In my experience this is one of the most amicable options for a divorce. You are not required to sling mud or assert inflammatory allegations at your spouse. The downside to this option is that it only applies after living separately for two years, so you must prolong the inevitable for two years once you have decided your marriage is over, which is not always that advantageous for those who want to reach a swift resolution to their financial separation and move on with their lives, and depending on what you do during those two years, it has the potential to be confusing for your children, if you have them.

While you can come to an arrangement between yourselves about your finances while you await the elapse of the two-year period (and this same advice applies to five years' separation, see page 44), your financial settlement is not final and both parties' claims against the other remain open until you are granted a legal divorce and court approved financial order setting out the terms of your financial agreement (see Chapter 13). Your own financial agreement would be persuasive if, after two years, you or your spouse applied for a divorce, and one of you tried to change your financial settlement, like having a second bite of the cherry. However, your financial agreement is not binding and there is a risk that another decision is made about your financial separation two years after you thought you had already agreed it. Commonly this is because:

- The spouses have not dealt with all of their matrimonial assets, for example they might have agreed what to do with their house, but didn't deal with their pension assets.

- An agreement reached at the time of separation, usually without the benefit of legal advice from one or both spouses, is unfair or not properly entered into (for example, full disclosure was not provided) and the court will not allow such an unfair settlement to be upheld.
- There has been a significant change in circumstances post-separation but before the divorce, which warrants a change to the terms of the financial agreement made at the time of separation.

Five years' separation

This is exactly what it says on the tin, and consent from your spouse is not required for this ground to be approved by the court. It's rarely used as most people do not want to wait for five years before they are able to divorce.

Desertion

Desertion is one of the lesser used grounds for a divorce. For you to rely on desertion, your spouse must have left you for a continuous period of at least two years with the intention that your relationship as husband and wife is over. In addition to this, the act of 'desertion' was done without you having behaved in such a way to reasonably warrant that reaction from your spouse. It must be against your wishes, meaning that you did not consent to your spouse leaving you. You can be deserted even if your spouse remains living in the same household as you, but you cannot continue to live as 'husband and wife'. The requirements to proving desertion are more complex than the other four options, and for those who have truly been left high and dry, locating the spouse who has 'deserted' can prove problematic.

The Divorce Process

Once you have decided upon which of the five facts you are going to use to prove that your marriage has irretrievably broken down, one of you needs to complete the court application form – the divorce petition – and become the 'petitioner'. The other spouse will be known as the 'respondent'. It may be possible for a joint application for a divorce to be made in the future. See page 57 in relation to the possible new divorce laws and this hopeful new option.

The benefit to being the petitioner is that you are the one who is slightly more in control of the process. You will have a couple more forms to complete than your spouse as the respondent, but you are the one that can first trigger each of the three stages of the divorce. You cannot be the petitioner if it is agreed that you will divorce based on your unreasonable behaviour, your adultery or your desertion.

There is a three-stage process for an unchallenged divorce.

First stage: the petition

The petition is the first court form that needs to be completed. You can do this online via the government website or get a paper version. If you have a lawyer they can draft this with you so that you have the confidence of knowing that it has been completed properly and you have not unknowingly prejudiced your position. Court staff cannot legally advise you and will not help you to complete the form.

The petition requires basic information about each spouse: full names, current addresses, dates of birth and information about your wedding. You must lift the information about the location of your wedding exactly as it is written on your marriage certificate, and include the date. There are more complex questions that require answering, such as on what basis you and/ or your spouse qualify to apply for a divorce in England and Wales, but it is, in the main, a tick box form, so the answers are provided – you just have to tick which one relates to your situation. If you have had a gradual separation over a period of time, you might want to give some thought to the date you give as your date of separation on the petition (see page 45 for more information about this). Getting the answers wrong can be a lengthy and potentially costly point to correct, so don't rush through it and take legal advice if you have any unusual aspects to your divorce, such as not having lived in England and Wales for some time.

Once you have a first draft of your petition it is recommended that you send it to your spouse so that they have an opportunity to review it and check their details have been completed correctly. This pre-sharing of the draft petition is particularly important when relying on adultery or unreasonable behaviour as the ground for divorce. You want to know that your spouse will not contest the adultery, or that your spouse approves your proposed examples of their unreasonable behaviour. If they object to any examples of their unreasonable behaviour, my advice is to be pragmatic and be seen to resolve their concerns. A slight redraft may go some way to helping you both to be amicable and starts the process off on a better footing. In my experience, this part of the process, albeit optional, can be a real marker in the sand for how the rest of the case will proceed. For example, if there is a fall out over the draft examples of unreasonable behaviour, then the tone of communication between spouses, and in some cases even their ability to communicate with each other at all, takes a nosedive and is difficult to repair.

To start the divorce process by post, the divorce petition (along with photocopies for the court file, one for your spouse and, if you've named a third person, a copy for them – this is a mandatory requirement), the marriage certificate and the court fee (which is, at the time of writing, £550, although there are some reductions available for those who might struggle to afford this), must be sent to the nearest court that deals with divorces, known as a 'divorce centre'. If using the online service, the government website explains how to submit the marriage certificate and pay the fee. The names of these 'divorce centres' are available online or you can check with your nearest court. Once the divorce petition has been sent to the divorce centre it will be 'issued'. This means the application will be allocated a case number, and that number will need to be quoted on all documents and correspondence thereafter in respect of the divorce and any financial matters (it is not used if you have any children's issues which are disputed in court, as a different case number will be allocated to that matter).

The divorce centre will send a notice to the petitioner to say that the application for the divorce has been issued along with a copy of the 'sealed' petition (one that has been rubber stamped and allocated a case number). A sealed petition will then be sent to the respondent spouse along with a form called an 'Acknowledgement of Service'. If someone has been named as part of an adultery allegation, that person will also be sent a copy of the issued petition.

The respondent has seven days from receipt of this form to complete it and return it to the divorce centre. It's not a long form and, in the main, requires only very short answers to questions such as 'What date did you receive the petition and at what address?'. The respondent has the opportunity on this form to state whether they intend on defending the petition.

My advice is that, unless you want to remain married to your spouse, think very carefully before you decide that you want to defend the petition. I explain more on page 52 about contested divorces. If you don't agree with what has been said about you by your spouse on their petition, try to be commercial in deciding whether it's worth a fight in contesting the divorce, when you do ultimately want a divorce. Is it worth the delay, admin and additional cost of getting them to amend their petition or in you cross-petitioning for a divorce on your own grounds against your spouse? These are all options, but are not necessarily appropriate or proportionate in many cases. Remember also that it is likely that you will need to resolve the arrangements for your children and financial matters, so choose your disputes (and therefore where you spend your money) wisely.

MONEY MATTERS

A couple of points to be aware of when starting your divorce process are related to money. On the divorce petition the petitioner is asked whether they wish to make an application for a financial order for themselves, and for any children. This does not mean that your financial issues are automatically started in court proceedings; it just means that you have indicated to the court that you have financial matters that also need resolving. It is normal to tick these boxes and failure to do so can later prejudice your case, so please do not fear them.

The second point relates to the costs of the divorce itself. The petitioner has the option of asking the court to make an order that requires the respondent to pay the costs they have incurred in obtaining the divorce. The costs of the divorce are limited only to the divorce and do not include the costs of sorting out your finances and/or any children or other issues. The costs can include the costs of a lawyer (for the divorce work only) and the costs of the court fee for issuing a divorce petition. The petitioner has the option of asking for all their costs or just a contribution towards their costs. In the Acknowledgement of Service form the respondent must state whether they agree to pay the costs asked for or, if not, why not. A common compromise position is to share the costs equally. The petitioner pays the court fee and has more work to do in the process than the respondent, so their legal costs will be higher if they have chosen to instruct a lawyer. Therefore, it can be considered fair for the respondent to contribute towards those costs. This can be another flashpoint at this early stage of the process, and it is important to carefully consider your position as to whether to apply for all your costs or just a contribution. It is best practice to let your spouse know about it before they receive the petition from the court.

Second stage: decree nisi

Once the Acknowledgement of Service has been returned to the divorce centre, a copy will be sent to the petitioner, which then enables the petitioner to apply for the middle stage of the divorce, known as the decree nisi. This is another straight-forward application form which you can obtain from the government's court forms website or from the court directly. 'Next steps' guidance information will also be sent to you by the court with each stage, and is also available on the government's divorce website.

The application for decree nisi is completed by the petitioner and sent to the divorce centre. On this form you must confirm that you still want a divorce and that the reasons for your divorce remain accurate. A judge will then review your application and your spouse's Acknowledgement of Service and decide whether you are entitled to a divorce. You will be informed by the court of the date on which a judge will pronounce your decree nisi, which means that a judge has entitled you to divorce. However, importantly, you are not yet divorced. The judge will also decide whether the respondent should pay for your costs of the divorce, if you requested this on your petition.

Neither you, your spouse or your legal representatives are required to attend the divorce centre for the pronouncement of your decree nisi, unless the respondent is contesting it. You will both receive your decree nisi in the post.

Third stage: decree absolute

As long as no application has been made to withdraw the application for a divorce, the earliest point at which a

DIVORCE OR DISSOLUTION OF YOUR CIVIL PARTNERSHIP

CHANGING YOUR MIND

It is rare that people make the big decision to seek a divorce then subsequently change their minds, but it does happen. Your marriage is not ended, and therefore you are not divorced, until you obtain a decree absolute from the court. You can stop the divorce process at any point up to decree absolute being pronounced by a judge in court. The divorce process actually has a built-in reflection period, as you are required to wait at least six weeks between the mid-stage of the divorce – the pronouncement of decree nisi – and applying for decree absolute.

petitioner can apply for decree absolute is six weeks and a day after the pronouncement of decree nisi. This involves another application form (available from the government's court forms website, and explained to you with the divorce 'next steps' guidance information you will receive from the court). Again, neither you nor your spouse is required to attend court. If the petitioner does not apply for decree absolute, a respondent can apply for it, but only after three months has passed since the petitioner was able to apply for it themselves.

Once decree absolute has been pronounced your marriage is dissolved. You will need to retain the original decree absolute, and it is advisable to hold copies which have been certified too, as this will be the document you use to provide evidence of your change in marital status and to change your name if you wish.

It is not normally advised that you apply for decree absolute until you have reached a financial settlement for potential tax reasons and also due to either spouse dying before financial matters are resolved. I explain more about this in Chapter 13.

Contested Divorce Proceedings

To defend a petition means the respondent either does not agree to the basis upon which a divorce is sought against them or that they do not agree to a divorce at all. To contest a divorce, the respondent must detail their reasons for objecting in accordance with the strict legal timelines and forms which must be kept to. If they are not adhered to, it can affect the success of any such contest. A contesting respondent must state on the Acknowledgement of Service that they wish to contest the divorce. In addition they must complete an Answer, which is a narrative explanation describing their reasons for their contest, and do so within a short deadline of 21 days from the date they must submit their Acknowledgement of Service to the court, along with payment of a court fee (which is, at the time of writing, £245). If a respondent fails to comply with the further procedural requirements of contesting, the petitioner can continue to pursue the divorce in the absence of the respondent's proper compliance. A judge may be willing to accommodate slight delays or mishaps in this process if the attempt to contest is genuine, but be warned that you are expected to keep to the timelines and produce the necessary documentation to explain why you contest the divorce, and to do so on time.

If you wish to contest the divorce purely because you don't agree with the ground for divorce used by your spouse, or you don't agree with the unreasonable behaviour examples they have set out in their petition, it is possible for you to ask your spouse to amend their petition (which will incur a fee and cause a slight delay to the process) or file your own petition (known as a 'cross petition' which will lead to a contested situation). Another option is to simply allow it to proceed but preserve your position by noting your objections on your Acknowledgement of Service form, while stating that, despite your objections, you agree to the divorce proceeding. It is useful to bear in mind the end goal here – if you agree that you want a divorce then contesting the detail is not particularly helpful, as the end goal is the same. Unless the allegations you or your spouse want to allege are serious enough to affect your arrangements for your children or financial settlement, then consider whether it is proportionate for you to contest the divorce.

For clients who struggle with this and feel strongly about correcting their spouse, it can help to understand that a divorce petition is not a public document. It is a private document between you, your spouse, your lawyers (if you have them) and the court. It is not a document that anyone else will be able to access and is certainly not something that will be shown to your children. Once you have decree absolute pronounced (the document that formally dissolves your marriage), you will not need to refer to the divorce petition again. The only document you will need going forward to evidence your divorce is the decree absolute. The decree absolute will state the ground for divorce but will not include the details, such as the examples of unreasonable behaviour. However, if you contest the divorce, you will need to have a court hearing where you each put forward your opinions and a judge will decide. If the contesting respondent is not successful, they are likely to be ordered to pay their petitioner spouse's legal fees for that hearing, which will be expensive, as well as their own legal fees, so it is not a process to pursue lightly.

DIY Divorce

I am aware that there are many online providers that offer to do your divorce for you. My only experience of these is when clients have attempted to use them and have subsequently had issues, which then drove them to spend money on a 'real-life' lawyer to unravel those issues. The government website (and just so you do not confuse it with any other online providers, the website will end '.gov.uk') has launched an online service for divorce. To use another online provider of a divorce is not something that I would recommend unless you know that the provider is genuinely regulated by the Solicitors Regulation Authority (as all practising lawyers and law firms are) and has someone accessible to you for advice and assistance. My understanding is a lot of 'online providers' simply act as prompts by telling you what information to input, but do not then consider your answers, decide whether what you have said is appropriate, chase the court for you if there are delays or if there is an error, or advise you on the likely questions you will have about the process.

Even if you intend on completing the process yourself, I recommend taking the advice of a family lawyer so that you receive guidance and advice on the best route for you, the wording you should use and the correct boxes you should or should not complete. Court staff are not able to give you legal advice, whether you use the online portal or the paper system through the court yourself.

If you choose to deal with your divorce by yourself, you must remember that your divorce does not settle your financial issues. As spouses you have financial rights and potential claims against each other. I explain more about these financial claims in Chapter 13, but what is really important to remember here is that divorcing each other alone does not bring those financial claims against each other to an end. Likewise, simply coming to an agreement between you about how to split your finances does not formally end those potential claims against each other either. The only way each of your financial claims can be fully settled in law, is for there to be a court order made which sets out the terms of your financial settlement. This can be achieved on paper by agreement and does not mean you have to battle each other through court. If you do not obtain a court order to formalise your financial settlement, you leave yourself open to having to deal with it in later years, so it is much better to take care of it all at once so that you can fully move on with your life without any worries about the past coming back up in your future.

If you have a particular reason why you do not want to formalise your financial settlement now, I would recommend discussing that reason with a family lawyer as it is likely that it can be dealt with now. For example, an agreement to delay the sale of the family home until your children finish their secondary school education can be agreed and reflected in a court order now setting out what will happen in the future. A financial order can be made at the same time as your divorce to reflect those decisions you have made now, even if they are not scheduled to occur until a future date.

International Couples and Considerations

It might be that the laws of England and Wales are more generous or advantageous to you when resolving your financial matters than if you were to deal with your financial separation in another country. It is better for you to have your divorce here if you also want the laws here to apply to your financial separation, although it can be possible to resolve your finances under our laws having divorced in another country. Likewise, it might be that it would be better for you if you could prevent our laws being applied in your financial settlement, and therefore you might want to find out if you can divorce elsewhere in the world. This can become a race to court, and timing really does matter. You will not be able to determine this issue on your own, so you will need to take advice quickly from an expert family lawyer. Speed and the right lawyer are of the essence here.

Our laws cover England and Wales and we are frequently referred to as 'the divorce capital of the world' because our laws are wide-ranging and discretionary when it comes to resolving marital finances on divorce, and are thought to be more generous than other countries. However, it is not as easy as just deciding that you want to take advantage of those perceived more favourable laws; you must make sure that the courts in England and Wales have what is known as 'jurisdiction' for your divorce and financial matters to take place here, and that means that you must show a sufficient connection (there are set requirements in law) to England and Wales.

Jurisdiction can be a complex issue and, if you have any international aspects to your marriage, you should make sure that you have discussed those with a specialist family lawyer (not all family lawyers will be experienced in international family law) before you start divorce proceedings anywhere in the world. An international aspect may be where you have lived abroad during your marriage, there are assets in another country or if you and/or your spouse are a different nationality to British but have a connection to England and Wales.

For a couple with international factors, choosing the right jurisdiction is likely to be a very important issue that must be carefully considered with an expert family lawyer, not only in this country but also in any other country which might also be able to deal with your divorce and financial matters. If you have taken the advice of an expert family lawyer they should be able to utilise their international network to obtain advice for you from family lawyers in the other countries in which you have connections to determine which country could deal with your divorce and financial proceedings, and which would be the best option for you.

Divorce, Dissolution and Separation Act 2019 – Expected Soon

At the time of writing, a new law has been debated and passed the initial phases through parliament to becoming law, and it is hoped that it will become law as soon as the end of 2019. If you are reading this book after that period then it is likely that these new provisions apply to you and I recommend checking out the government website to confirm your options for divorce in light of this new law at www.gov.uk/divorce.

This new proposed law is intended to take away the need for spouses to lay blame in order to prove that their relationship has irretrievably broken down, make the process smoother, more amicable (you can even apply together!) and therefore more cost efficient. In its current draft, the new law will allow a spouse alone or spouses jointly together to simply state that their marriage has broken down irretrievably. No more mud slinging, no accusations of adultery, or time spent living apart beforehand. That statement alone will be sufficient evidence for the court to progress your divorce without contest from your spouse. In divorce cases, the court will make a conditional order to end the marriage after this statement is given.

This order cannot be made final without the applicant, or applicants if it was a joint application, confirming their wish for it to be made final. There will be an enforced waiting period, to give spouses time to reflect before their marriage is finally ended. The confirmation that a spouse or the spouses want the order to be made final cannot be given until at least 20 weeks after the date the application was first made for a divorce, and the divorce cannot be finalised until 6 weeks after the date of the conditional order, after which the marriage will be ended.

For those seeking a judicial separation, the 20-week waiting period will not apply and the statement by one or both spouses that they wish to be judicially separated will be enough for the court to make such an order final immediately.

PART III

IF YOU CAN'T AGREE

CHAPTER 4

Communicating Directly
with Your Ex

N EARLY ALL MY clients experience some issues with communicating with their ex-partner. My advice is always to proceed with caution and with an amicable approach in mind. I understand that, in reality, you might not feel particularly amicable at times, or at all, so it is going to be hard to take a conciliatory approach when proceeding with your separation. High-conflict situations are common in cases involving adultery, substance misuse, or where financial misconduct is suspected of one spouse, such as them having hidden money. However, it's so important to try to limit your emotional responses to the process and view each decision with a commercial-like mind in order to filter through to the important issues at hand. The way in which your separation is dealt with will have a huge impact on your ongoing relationship with your spouse and has a high chance of having a knock-on effect on how you settle your finances and any issues relating to your children. And your ongoing relationship is so important when you have children together – I cannot stress this enough. You will have an ongoing relationship with your ex-partner even when your separation and financial settlement are finalised and it will make your lives, and your children's lives, so much easier if you can come out the other side at least able to be civil with each other.

If you are struggling to communicate with your ex-partner, there is a sliding scale of what you can try in order to overcome that difficulty. The first is to change how you communicate with each other. You can try counselling together, not necessarily with the purpose of trying to reconcile, but as a means of you discussing how best to communicate. This is particularly advantageous for couples who have children together and really do need to learn how to communicate so that they can co-parent. However, you cannot force someone to go to counselling with you, so this won't be an option for everyone.

Changing the way in which you communicate can really help. If you find that when you talk face-to-face or on the phone you end up in an argument, being shouted at or being interrupted and not getting to finish your point, stop talking face-to-face or on the phone about the issues that you know cause conflict. Instead, switch to communicating about those issues via text message (for short communications) or email, and keep those communications to 'business hours' only. By communicating in this way, you give yourself time to think about what you want to say, the tone you use and the way in which you explain your views or make your proposals. Your ex-partner cannot interrupt you, so you can make sure that you finish your point and fully respond to theirs. You can write a draft and go back to it later when you're in a different mood. You can even ask a friend, relative or family lawyer to 'sense check' it for you before you press 'send'.

The other benefit of this is that you can write your knee-jerk response, get your anger out, say what your instinct tells you to say and benefit from having written down your feelings. But do not send it! Save it to your drafts (and never to be sent) file, send it to your best mate, or even to your family lawyer, but never send it to your ex-partner. Just enjoy knowing that you've got it off your chest, and then go on to draft the appropriate, considered and more amicable real response.

By keeping the communications between the hours of 9am and 6pm you can avoid those middle of the night angry rants or drunken text messages. You should let your ex-partner know these boundaries and say that, for the time being, you would like for both of you to communicate via email only and during business hours. You should, of course, say that in an emergency they can text or call, particularly if you have children together. If their contact with you is abusive or harassing then you should consider whether more serious action needs to be taken, such as involving the police and/or instructing a family lawyer to write to them requesting that their behaviour stops (see Chapter 7).

The business hours and email/text-only switch up is a great option for those who feel that there is a power imbalance in their relationship and are used to feeling dominated in direct talks. It might feel a bit extreme to put such a wall up about communication, but if your ex-partner respects your request, it might help to calm the situation, allow you to both air your views in a considered manner and then, if you feel able once matters have calmed and stabilised, you can go back to talking to each other directly again.

Be assertive and change your previous role stereotypes

You might have found that both you and your ex-partner had certain roles and personality traits which defined you during your relationship. It is possible that those characteristics were part of the cause of the breakdown of your relationship, and possibly magnified by your dispute. Being the more dominant person may make it very difficult for you to now be challenged and accept there are other ways of doing things. Being the more submissive personality in your relationship is likely to make it difficult for you to now be more assertive. I often meet clients who tell me their reasonable and sensible views but say that they are struggling to communicate those views to their more dominant ex-partner. Changing the more extreme previous relationship stereotypes will need to take place if you are to successfully move forward with your dispute and, if applicable, co-parent your children post-separation.

Post-separation there is often an absence of trust and feelings of hurt and fear of the unknown. A more dominant personality might be able to bluff their way through these feelings by telling their ex-partner their interpretation of 'what's fair' and say it with such confidence, often buoyed by the words 'my lawyer says' (the truth of which I am rarely convinced), to give force to their opinion. This can be very intimidating to the submissive personality and makes it hard for them to challenge. Try to bear in mind that your ex-partner is probably being like that out of habit and out of fear of the unknown.

You can help yourself to be more assertive and have more presence in the dispute by doing two things. Firstly, where appropriate to the type of dispute, take legal advice, even if it's just a one-off meeting. A meeting with a family lawyer should be long enough and detailed enough to give you a good indication of the bracket within which you might reasonably settle your dispute, and your options for how you might achieve that. You can then go back to your ex-partner with confidence in your opinions. It will give you a much more stable platform from which to voice your views, and give you some boundaries within which you can more comfortably make compromises. You have reduced your fear of the unknown by informing yourself of the potential outcomes.

Secondly, with your newly increased confidence you can give assurances, which will help you to be more assertive. When you both fear the unknown and lose trust in one another, you usually end up with neither of you willing to budge because the reality is that neither of you really know what the answer should be or whether the other is being reasonable. The fear factor can blur reasonableness and by giving some reassurance, such as 'I am not going to take the children away from you; I will always encourage their relationship with you' or 'I am not going to stop paying into our joint account; I will continue to meet the existing outgoings', you might find that it helps your informed voice to be heard by alleviating some of their fear.

For the submissive character, finding your informed voice is the first step and then it is a matter of choosing the best method of communicating that to your ex-partner. Asserting yourself does not mean you should do it verbally, and I recommend that you follow my advice about switching how you communicate to emails, for example, so that a less assertive person can be read, if not heard.

Pick your battles

It can be difficult to take a step back from your dispute with your ex-partner and know which battles are worth fighting, especially when you are carrying the emotional baggage of your relationship history. The best advice I can give you is to think about whether the point to be made or responded to will make any difference to the overall outcome or if it is significant enough to pursue. It is not always black and white. Will arguing about paying for the children's new school uniform make a difference to the overall outcome? It is unlikely, but the cost may not be inconsequential and so it might be a significant enough issue to make it worth raising. Arguing about being slightly late to hand over your children on one occasion is not worth pursuing. You should note it down in your diary, but it is probably not, in isolation, going to make a difference to the overall outcome.

It is easy to get pulled into tit-for-tat-style disputes as mainly they come down to setting the record straight – correcting the other in their version of events, which are stated as fact, causing you to feel it necessary to put forward your own account. Try to stay focused on the significant or imminent issues and don't respond at all to all the other noise.

Think also about the timing of your disputes. Is it worthwhile engaging in communications with your ex-partner that are likely to rock the boat if you know that a bigger issue will need to be raised just around the corner? For example, if you know that you will need to talk about the arrangements for your children for Christmas or whether you will retain the matrimonial home as part of your settlement, it will not assist you to start or respond to any minor issues which will just use up emotion, energy and time and distract from the bigger issues. The minor disputes will do damage to the amicability of your relationship, which is hard to rebuild, and they serve little purpose if, when it comes to the big decisions, you are harbouring negativity from those prior minor issues.

I know it is easier said than done, but it will greatly assist you to be able to draw a line under the less significant issues which provoke an emotional response in you and move on. If you need to get some external assistance from a counsellor or therapist to do this, then do it to help yourself. The benefit to you in learning how to control how you respond to your ex-partner, and understanding which battles to pick and which to drop, could be the key to the success of your settlement terms and, if applicable, your ongoing co-parenting relationship.

Use intermediaries

If you have any mutual friends or family members who are particularly fond of you both, they might be quite useful intermediaries. It's quite a burden to ask a third party to be a go-between, but as a one-off it might be a real help to have someone you both trust talk to each of you and communicate your views to the other. They can control the tone and the way those views are communicated, which will reduce the inflammation between you. However, not everyone is comfortable with introducing third parties into their separation because of the social awkwardness, and there is a risk that it might not help if they are viewed as biased or if they overstep the mark (albeit in an attempt to genuinely help). I have had a number of cases where a parent has stepped in as a communicator, and it has helped to keep communications respectful and purposeful (for example, specifically about the arrangements for the children). However, I have also dealt with many cases where a parent's intervention has done nothing but inflame the situation.

My warning about utilising third parties, beyond any social awkwardness, is where they might be conflicted by financial matters. For example, many parents have helped their children get onto the property ladder by giving them a lump sum. Though this might have occurred many years ago, it may become an issue as part of the financial settlement, so parents could be viewed as biased when it comes to being an intermediary and may be conflicted if their evidence later also becomes required. Similarly, a best friend may also be a business partner, and that business will form part of your finances to consider in your financial settlement. Therefore it's important to consider whether that best friend/business partner is really the right person to be asked to assist you both right now. New partners are also a 'Marmite' person to involve. Sometimes, new partners can assist in handovers of children where you and your ex-partner struggle to do it yourself, but the emotion invoked by the presence of a new partner can also mean that they can greatly inflame the situation.

The third-party option is only really viable for the short term to help calm a situation or to deal with imminent issues, and choosing the right intermediary is vital for this option's success.

If you have got to the point where you feel that you have tried all you can to communicate with your ex-partner but your views are simply not being heard and you find that you are too far apart in your positions for you to be able to make any further progress on your own, the next step should be for you to either self-refer to mediation or instruct your family lawyer to write to your ex-partner on your behalf. You can combine both, and instruct a lawyer to write and, as part of that letter, invite your ex-partner to attend mediation with you. These alternative options for resolving disputes, along with arbitration and collaborative law, are explained in the next chapter.

CHAPTER 5

Non-Court Dispute Resolution Options

A T ANY POINT of your dispute it is worth considering alternative options for resolving your issues:

- negotiation (direct between yourselves or via family lawyers)
- mediation
- collaborative law
- arbitration

These are 'alternative' options because they are done with the view that you can resolve your dispute and avoid court. They can be used in all types of family law disagreements, from children's issues to resolving your financial settlement on divorce. Using non-court dispute resolution can be emotional and at times difficult, but the processes should be time- and cost-effective and keep you and your ex-partner at the forefront of the decision-making process, so that the two of you are the ones that decide what happens to you and/or your family.

Negotiation

We have already discussed how to improve the communications between you and your ex-partner either directly or via a trusted mutual person, which might enable you to then negotiate between yourselves (see Chapter 4). If you choose this option I cannot place enough emphasis on taking the advice of a family lawyer before you enter negotiations about any significant disputes. The reason for this is because any offers or concessions you make during those negotiations, while made in a genuine attempt to settle your dispute, will become part of the history of your dispute and will likely be referenced or even relied upon later by your ex-partner if those initial direct negotiations are unsuccessful. You therefore run the risk of prejudicing your case if you later end up in court. Taking legal advice at the outset of your dispute might prove invaluable and place you in a better starting position from which you can negotiate for yourself.

If you have tried negotiating yourself, or if you do not want to attempt direct negotiations, you can ask a family lawyer to represent you and negotiate on your behalf through correspondence with your ex-partner or their lawyer, which may lead to a round-table meeting, using mediation or arbitration, or even in court proceedings. Whether your ex-partner also has representation from a family lawyer or whether they are unrepresented (also known as a 'litigant in person'), having your own family lawyer to negotiate on your behalf takes the pressure off you and means your position is presented with the right emphasis placed on your best points, the legal argument to support your case and the process correctly applied and/or explained.

Taking legal advice

I frequently have clients who have attempted to deal with their separation and related issues themselves in the hope that it will help to keep things civil, but often relationships can quickly deteriorate when there are unresolved issues. I find this is often due to a misunderstanding or lack of understanding. If you don't each have a family lawyer to explain your options and the process to you then it is easy for one or both of you to make mistakes along the way. Knowing when to focus on which issue and whether to engage in communications about the detail of those issues is difficult on your own due to your emotional involvement. Family lawyers can separate out the important issues and raise them in priority order or in relation to the stage at which you are in resolving your dispute.

There are a lot of common misconceptions about the law and relationship breakdowns, and it can be one or both of you believing these misconceptions which causes the conflict. Misconceptions such as 'a mother has more say about the children', 'a separated father will only see his children on alternate weekends' and 'I earned more than you, so I get to keep more' are frequently raised. Remember also that what happened to a friend or family member after their separation will not necessarily be applicable to you. If, even with family lawyers, you are in a high-conflict situation, some thought needs to be given about what has caused that conflict. Often the cause can be where one spouse does not agree that the marriage has broken down and does not want to engage in the process. The more you pursue it, the deeper they dig in their heels. At other times, the cause lies with emotions, and one of the spouses feeling angry or hurt.

If these emotions are overriding logic and reasonableness, couples often find themselves in high conflict. Getting bespoke family law advice will enable you to understand how the law applies in your particular circumstances. You can then use that knowledge to return to direct talks with your ex-partner or, if that option has been exhausted for now, you can ask your family lawyer to write to your ex-partner on your behalf to explain the process, any misunderstanding and, if appropriate at that stage, your proposals to resolve your dispute.

How to choose a family lawyer

There are thousands of lawyers in England and Wales, but not all of them are specialised in family law. Family lawyers may not all deal with divorce, children's disputes and financial settlements, so make sure you find one experienced in the type of family law that relates to your particular dispute(s). Ask for recommendations, look at the lawyer's online profile to see where their specific expertise lies, or even briefly speak to the lawyer on the phone if you can.

As a family lawyer, I think it's important to have a good relationship with my clients. Beyond me having the right legal expertise, it's also a personality match. Family law issues relate to matters of the heart and, whether that is the end of your relationship or issues relating to your children and co-parenting, they are emotive issues to discuss and often make clients feel vulnerable. Intimate details about your relationship and parenting may need to be discussed, and sometimes clients are entrusting me with information that they have not even discussed with their family or closest friends. Therefore, it is important that you feel comfortable with your family lawyer, are able to communicate with them freely and feel like they understand you.

I recommend looking for a family lawyer who is a member of Resolution, which means they have signed up to representing their clients in accordance with a code of conduct to resolve disputes as amicably as possible, with the focus on the children to make sure their needs are put first. Finding a family lawyer who is also a member of Resolution is easy as there is a 'Find a Member' section on its website and you can search in reference to your location (see www.resolution.org.uk).

While it is likely that affordability will be a priority consideration for you when looking for a family lawyer, matching the right level of experience to the complexity of your dispute is also something you should consider. Experience does not always mean the overall cost is more as long as it is proportionate to the difficulty of your case. Though you will pay more for a more experienced lawyer, that more experienced lawyer will be best placed to deal with more complex issues. For more straightforward disputes, an experienced lawyer will deal with those issues concisely (and therefore take less time) or supervise junior team members who then charge a lower hourly rate. Your family lawyer will give you an estimate of costs for dealing with each of your issues. It is difficult to be precise at the beginning of your dispute as the time spent in resolving your issues will depend on how well your ex-partner engages in the process, the extent of the disputes between you and what might be required to resolve them, such as expert evidence.

For more complex issues, or if you have multiple issues in dispute, it is likely to be preferable for you to have a family lawyer who works in a law firm that also has departments covering different areas of law. For example, if you have been separated from your partner but never married and you have a dispute over your house, it would be better if your family lawyer has, should it become necessary, a property litigation lawyer they can work with to combine their expertise and give you the best advice and representation. The same applies if you have a business in contention – a family lawyer, corporate lawyer, and perhaps even an employment lawyer, might be needed on your team of advisors. If your family lawyer works in a firm that only offers family law services, please don't worry, they will likely have connections with other lawyers and they should still be able to work together for you.

Keep in mind that, for the majority of lawyers, they charge on a time spent basis, which means that the more time they spend working on your case the more time will be charged to you. If you contact your lawyer over email, remember that your lawyer must read that email, and it will usually require your lawyer to act. The communication in (of any form) and consequential actions out are all time spent on your case. The best use of your lawyer is for legal advice (I know that sounds obvious, but bear with me) and the legal drafting of letters and documents. Due to the emotive and personal nature of family law, clients often talk to their lawyers about those extra issues, some of which will be legally relevant, but sometimes they won't. Be mindful of calling or emailing your lawyer to complain about your ex-partner and make sure that the information you provide to your lawyer is appropriate to your dispute and focused on the legal issues at hand. You won't always know whether information is relevant or not, so float the topic swiftly and your lawyer will advise whether they need to know more.

LEGAL AID

There are limited circumstances where legal aid is available to assist with funding or fund outright family law disputes, and in the main it remains available where there has been or is domestic abuse, and where you are unable to fund legal fees from your own resources. If you want to look into whether legal aid might be available to your dispute and if you are eligible I recommend going to https://www.gov.uk/check-legal-aid.

I have also experienced clients who try to minimise their legal fees to such an extent that they prevent me from being able to properly advise and represent them. It is very hard to represent a client if too many restrictions are put in place, such as saying 'I want you to advise me about this question only' and therefore expecting your lawyer to limit their advice to a specific point, when usually it requires consideration of the whole dispute and the many intertwined issues involved. To restrict your lawyer too much also has the potential to mean that they cannot fully 'act in your best interest' which is a standard required of them by the Law Society. Lawyers can be instructed for limited or specific tasks, but to over-restrict is unlikely to be of benefit to you. A comparison would be to seek medical assistance about a back problem, only informing the doctor of the pain but preventing them from an examination or scan. They are aware there is an issue but full investigation is prevented so the outcome and the assistance are limited. No one benefits from these too-restrictive types of instructions.

How to work with your lawyer

The best advice is to listen to your lawyer. I appreciate that you might find yourself overloaded with information and it can be difficult to take it all in. In which case, you should either request a note from your lawyer, take your own notes or take someone with you to also listen to the advice and take notes for you (all of these options combined is best!). Ignoring your lawyer's advice is a costly exercise and usually creates more work for them. They will probably have to repeat previously given advice and also try to undo any damage caused by their advice having not been taken on board. Be prepared that your lawyer may not tell you what you want to hear. However, their advice will hopefully reset your expectations and put you on a more reasonable track to settlement. Where you can, do as much of the layman's work as possible, such as liaising with mediators about appointments or compiling your financial disclosure documents. You should also keep your lawyer in the loop about your own updates and timescales. This will help to keep the costs down.

I think it is best to have a full and detailed initial meeting with a lawyer to discuss your options for next steps and a plan of action. Before you attend that meeting, you should write out a chronology detailing important information about your relationship history and progression, your finances and your children. Include information relevant to your dispute, so if it is about arrangements for your children, state what the arrangements are currently and what you and your ex-partner each want to change. State what you know of your financial position, your joint finances and your partner/ex-partner's finances. Make a note of all the questions you want answered. Email this information, along with any existing court documents or agreements or noteworthy correspondence, to your lawyer ahead of your meeting. If your lawyer can spend a bit of time reading in to your case ahead of your initial meeting it will allow them to focus your meeting on the right issues and make it more effective.

Once you have been advised of your options and suggested plan of action, you can decide whether you want to be fully represented, have your lawyer in the background as support for you only or try to resolve things on your own. Your lawyer will not be offended if you want to try to resolve matters on your own or if you just want to keep them in the background. It is common for people to attend an initial meeting and not need the lawyer's assistance again at all, or until some months or even a year or more later. It is your case and you make all the decisions. Striking the right balance and plan of action which is appropriate to your dispute and affordability is part of working as a team with your lawyer.

> Your lawyer will inform you if they intend on closing your file. This simply means that your file is sent to storage (usually offsite) and they do not expect to undertake any further work for you. You can at any time reinstruct your lawyer and as long as it is within seven years of your last instruction, your file can be recalled back from storage. This is not normally chargeable.

Getting legal advice also helps you to set your own expectations. For your ex-partner, receiving a lawyer's letter can also help to set their expectations with a greater understanding of your position and how you want to resolve the issues. Bringing formality to your dispute by having a family lawyer correspond on your behalf can signal a change – it can be a sign that you are taking things seriously and want to make progress in resolving your dispute. Sometimes people are not ready to bring such a change to their dealings with their ex-partner, for fear that it may heighten the tensions between them, and worry about the snowball effect. However, just because you now have a family lawyer acting for you does not mean that you will end up at court or that you and your ex-partner have to stop your own communications. A lot of my clients are able to resolve their disputes through their family lawyer's correspondence and negotiations. Sometimes this is done in conjunction with non-court alternative dispute resolution, for example continuing negotiations direct between ex-partners, or alongside mediation or arbitration.

If you have reached the point of instructing a family lawyer, there are lots of options available to you to resolve your dispute with your ex-partner. A good start will often be a more formal email or letter to your ex-partner or their family lawyer, either from you or your family lawyer. In the appropriate circumstances, I frequently encourage clients to keep their correspondence between them but I assist my clients in writing that correspondence. This can mean that I 'ghostwrite' it for them or they write it for my review. If it is decided that I should write on my client's behalf, I always draft letters with my clients' input and final approval before they are sent. You know your ex-partner better than your family lawyer and working together on letters ensures the content and the tone are set appropriately. This way of working with your family lawyer also keeps you fully involved. Informing your family lawyer of practical points helps you to work as a team and approach your ex-partner in the best way, for example, telling your family lawyer not to send a letter on a particular day, such as a special occasion, when you know they are on holiday or a day before a weekend your children will be with them.

Receiving a letter from a family lawyer on behalf of your ex-partner, whether expected or not, can be a bit of a reality check. It is advisable to let your ex-partner know in advance to expect a letter, but do so in a friendly and non-threatening way. By communicating this to them it can help the amicability of the relationship between you. However, it will not always be appropriate to give advance warning, so you should discuss with your family lawyer the best approach in light of your circumstances and the content of the letter to be sent.

I always tell my clients that one of the best things their ex-partner can do is to take their own legal advice from a family lawyer. If you encourage your ex-partner to take their own advice it means they will be advised on the law and how it applies to them, and should therefore help to adjust any unreasonable views they might be naively holding which have become a sticking point between you. I do, unfortunately, find myself repeating to clients the old saying 'You can lead a horse to water but you can't make it drink'. A stubborn unreasonable person will be difficult to help, but that's not to say you shouldn't try. Remember that you and your ex-partner cannot see the same family lawyer because the lawyer will be conflicted in advising you both. I can understand that it sounds like a good idea to go together and hear the same advice together, but lawyers are simply not allowed to do this due to the potential for conflict.

Family lawyers will usually progress your case through correspondence with your ex-partner or their family lawyer and can then enter into negotiations on your behalf either through letters/emails, over the phone or in a round-table meeting. A round-table meeting is where you and your ex-partner both attend with your family lawyers and see if you can make progress, narrow the issues between you and, where possible, reach settlement terms. This can be quite attractive to those who prefer to have their family lawyer with them in a meeting with their ex-partner. Your family lawyer can advise you throughout and progress your case, give you advice on the law and your best-/worst-case scenario which will be reviewed as your case progresses. This may also include obtaining advice from a barrister who will give a second opinion and work as part of your team of advisors to make strategic decisions on progressing your case. Your family lawyer will signpost you to non-court resolution options as and when they might be appropriate during your case, and will also advise you on when court proceedings become appropriate, or how to deal with them should your ex-partner start them.

Mediation

As I have recommended, taking early legal advice, even if it is just a one-off, is really going to help you to resolve your dispute. Sometimes people direct themselves straight to mediation, which is very positive and something to be encouraged, but, as a mediator cannot provide you with legal advice, I would recommend that you take legal advice before your session and in between sessions, if necessary. This does mean that you will incur the costs of your family lawyer as well as the cost of the mediator, but it is vital to go into mediation with the confidence of knowing that you have talked through your position, you understand the law which supports your position and you have a good idea in your mind of where there is room for manoeuvre, while still achieving the outcome you want.

Mediation is a process by which you and your ex-partner (without your family lawyers with you) attend a meeting with a mediator to discuss what the issues are in dispute between you and attempt to narrow the gap between your respective positions, and hopefully reach a settlement. Choosing the right mediator will be key to the process and you can ask your family lawyer for recommendations. A mediator is an independent person, so they cannot have already been involved in your dispute. This means that a family lawyer that either you or your ex-partner have taken advice from in the past (even informally) or who is currently advising, cannot mediate between you. For family disputes, I always recommend using a mediator who is also a family lawyer as they have a good understanding of the legal processes. The mediator will not be able to legally advise either of you but they can help to guide you through the issues and keep those negotiations between you calm, focused and appropriate.

The first session is usually to understand the issues in dispute and to set out an idea of what you both want to achieve. The mediator will then help you to agree what information you both need to provide for the next session and help you each understand your perspectives. If you are attending mediation to discuss the relocation of your children, for example, perhaps that required information would be about the schools and housing available in the new area. If you are attending mediation to discuss a financial settlement, you will need to provide disclosure of your respective financial positions, such as your bank statements, and set out your estimated needs going forward in terms of monthly expenditure and capital requirements for such things as housing, a car, furnishings and retraining.

There is no limit on how many mediation sessions you can attend. It might be that you only need two or three sessions for simpler disputes, while more complex disputes will likely require more. A mediator charges an hourly rate which you can either both contribute towards or agree that one of you will solely fund. Sometimes mediators' fees are covered by legal aid and you can locate a mediator close to you and enquire as to the availability of mediation by going to https://www.familymediationcouncil.org.uk/find-local-mediator/. Mediation can be a cost- and time-effective process, with meetings arranged fairly swiftly and regularly so that your dispute is not unnecessarily dragged out. You and your ex-partner make the decisions which means you retain autonomy over how your dispute is progressed and settled.

The additional benefit of mediation is that your discussions are 'without prejudice', which means that you can make concessions about your position in an attempt to settle your dispute, with the protection of knowing that it cannot then be referred to 'openly' in any later (out of mediation) correspondence or court proceedings. It gives you both the freedom of letting your guard down with the security of not later prejudicing your case should a settlement not be reached during mediation.

It can be difficult to go into mediation without your family lawyer to make your points for you and, for some, knowing the nature of their ex-partner, this task is simply too daunting. In a situation where you are used to being talked over or dominated by your ex-partner you might be unwilling to try mediation, but there are still mediation options that are worth considering. Some mediators work in pairs, so there are two mediators to assist the process, which helps to even out the numbers and make the sessions feel more equal, and to control the discussions. Another option which can be attractive to those who fear being dominated, but also where relations have broken down to such an extent that you can't bear to be in the same room as each other or for your own protection, is 'shuttle mediation'. You and your ex-partner are sat in separate rooms and the mediator 'shuttles' between you to progress the talks and negotiations in a controlled environment.

Mediation is a voluntary process that cannot be enforced upon either of you, so if one of you refuses to attend or attends but does not properly engage in the process then that's the end of mediation. Before court proceedings are started there is a requirement that the applicant, and the respondent (if they agree to attend), each attend what is called a 'Mediation Information and Assessment Meeting' (a 'MIAM'). A MIAM is a short (about 30 minutes), individual meeting with the mediator to discuss what mediation is, a brief overview of your dispute and whether mediation might be appropriate to resolving your issues. If after your MIAM you decide not to use mediation, or if you are prevented from using mediation because your ex-partner refuses to attend, the mediator will sign a form to say that the MIAM has been attended. You must have that signed form if you then want to make an application to court. There are exemptions to this requirement, such as where domestic abuse has occurred or if you or your ex-partner are now based a significant distance apart.

However, nowadays distance does not have to be a reason for you to discount mediation as some mediators are able to offer videoconferencing facilities.

Collaborative Law

For situations where you and your ex-partner both want to work together to resolve your dispute, but you also want the support of your lawyers, collaborative law might be a good option. You each instruct a family lawyer who is trained in collaborative law (not all family lawyers are) and the four of you agree to try to resolve your dispute together, predominantly by way of face-to-face meetings. The emphasis for this type of dispute resolution is to use those meetings to narrow your issues and reach resolution, rather than corresponding in writing or over the phone. The idea is that it can be quicker because you are all together and you and your ex-partner retain autonomy over how your issues are resolved.

If collaborative law does not work out for you then your respective family lawyers cannot continue to work for you. When you stop collaborative law you must each instruct new family lawyers if you continue to want legal representation. The reason for this is so that you feel like your family lawyer is just as invested as you in resolving your dispute via the collaborative process, as if the collaborative process breaks down, they lose their clients.

If you like the idea of having your respective family lawyers with you to discuss your dispute, then you can have a 'round-table meeting' at any point, and you do not need to specifically be part of the 'collaborative law' process. A well-timed round-table meeting can be a real breakthrough in settling your dispute as you are all sat together, with the benefit of legal advice, to sort out your issues.

Arbitration

Arbitration is a non-court dispute resolution option, but the difference with this option is that someone else makes the ultimate decisions for you. If you and your ex-partner are unable to reach an agreement between you, but you would still rather avoid going to court, then arbitration is likely to work well for you.

Each of your family lawyers can represent and assist you in the process, but instead of a judge in court making the decision for you, a trained arbitrator acts as the judge and decides for you, which you can then get transferred into a binding court order. There are a few important differences between arbitration and the court process, as well as some advantages to choosing arbitration for your dispute.

The court process can be long; in many cases, it can take over a year to complete before you even get to the point of being ready for a final hearing. The court process is also more rigid, requiring set structures and preliminary hearings before getting to a final hearing where a judge makes a final decision. The formality of being at court and in the courtrooms can also put some people off.

With arbitration, you, your family lawyers and the arbitrator agree the structure and process tailored to your dispute. You can use arbitration from the beginning to the end, to include the preliminary hearing stages and final hearing. Alternatively, you can arbitrate on a specific issue and then carry on negotiations yourselves, having gotten over a sticking point. Alternatively, if you and your family lawyers agree that you have done all the groundwork in narrowing the issues between you and obtained all the relevant information you require to enable a final decision to be made (such as each of your financial disclosures, and expert reports or valuations), you can appoint an arbitrator simply to make the final decision.

Arbitration should be considered throughout your progress. If you are mediating with your ex-partner but you are struggling to agree then you could use mediation to define the outstanding issues between you and use an arbitrator to decide those issues so that together you have reached an overall conclusion. I discuss arbitration with clients, say in financial matters, where they have gone through the first two court hearings and now face a long wait for a final hearing date with the court. It can be very useful at that stage to use arbitration to bring about a swifter resolution. The arbitration process can be moulded by you so that you can choose where to have it, how you want it to work (for example, have multiple arbitrations to decide preliminary issues first or just one final arbitration), who your arbitrator is and when you want it to take place. It fits how your dispute is working out and it is that bespoke level of service that can make it so effective in emotion, time and money.

Trained arbitrators tend to be experienced family lawyers and include solicitors, barristers and retired judges. You and your ex-partner will get to choose your own arbitrator, so you both can have the comfort of selecting an arbitrator who has appropriate experience in your type of dispute. If you go through the court process, you will, of course, be allocated a judge who deals with family law disputes, but you do not get to choose your judge for any stage hearing. The ability to make your own choice is particularly advantageous if you have a complexity to your case, such as a family business at the heart of your dispute, and you can therefore choose an arbitrator who has a lot of experience in handling those types of assets, or if your dispute is in relation to arrangements for your children, you can choose an arbitrator with experience in this area.

Time is also the big advantage here. The arbitrator is likely to be available within a matter of weeks as opposed to waiting for a final hearing in court which will not likely be for a matter of some months. The arbitrator will also have more time to dedicate to your case. Unfortunately, a judge in a court process is rather burdened by a heavy caseload which pressures the time they have available to prepare for your case. An arbitrator will make sure they have sufficient time ahead of hearing your case to undertake the appropriate reading so that they come to your hearing fully aware of your case, and understand the detail and intricacies of your dispute. This extra level of care and preparation that an arbitrator can have compared to a judge will make a lot of difference to you and potentially to the final outcome. You can receive the final decision having confidence that the arbitrator fully understood your case, therefore reducing the chances of you feeling discontented with the arbitrator's final decision and the dispute being prolonged any further. Speeding up the process, as long as all the information required to settle your dispute is available, will undoubtedly be advantageous to all involved.

The arbitrator's decision will be referred to as the 'award' in a financial case or the 'determination' in a matter relating to children. The arbitrator's decision will be binding against you and your ex-partner. For financial awards you must then turn it into a consent order to be approved by a judge in court, just as you would need to do if you reached agreement directly between yourselves, through lawyers or through mediation (see page 81). For a determination about a children's issue, it is up to you whether you also want it to be converted into a consent order. A judge is likely to approve the award made by an arbitrator and it should all be completed by post so you will not need to attend court.

Though, as we've seen, there are many advantages to arbitration, it does come with a price tag. You and your ex-partner will have to pay for the arbitrator in addition to your own representatives. The arbitrator will charge a fixed fee but the money saved by skipping the longer court process will make it cost-effective (if it is proportionate to the value of the assets or urgency involved in your case), and save you time, emotion and stress from your dispute being prolonged any further. Legal aid is not available for arbitration.

It's also worth noting that there are some restrictions to arbitration which means a few specific family law issues cannot be resolved by an arbitrator, such as if there are allegations of harm against a child. Your family lawyer will be able to advise you about your case's suitability for arbitration. For the majority of issues, arbitration will be available. It will come down to whether you and your ex-partner choose this route.

Obtaining a Consent Order

Whether you use direct negotiation, solicitor negotiation, mediation, collaborative law or arbitration to resolve your dispute, once you have agreed the terms of your settlement you can convert those agreed terms in an order for approval by the court, making it an enforceable court order. You can ask your family lawyer to draft what is called a 'consent order', so that the terms are properly set out and drafted to have the correct legal effect. If you have not used a family lawyer to negotiate your agreement, I recommend instructing one to draft the consent order for you. A consent order is vital to making sure your settlement is appropriately and finally secured between you, but it is a legal document that requires proper legal drafting. Once you and your ex-partner agree to the drafting of the consent order you can send it to the court for a judge to approve and make it a formal order of the court. You can do all this without actually needing to set foot in a court.

If your agreement is in relation to settling your finances on divorce then turning your settlement terms into a consent order should be considered as a mandatory action. If your agreement is in relation to arrangements for your children, a consent order is not a necessary action, but one which should be considered. I explain more about the obtaining a consent order in relation to arrangements for your children on page 151.

If you decide to divorce but fail to obtain a consent order to reflect what you agreed should happen with your finances then you leave yourself open to future claims from your ex-partner. Don't do all the hard work of reaching an agreement just to forget the formalities and then later regret it. While there are some safeguards in place in the law (for example, in a later claim a judge would consider any evidence you have to show why you understood that you had reached an agreement at the time), these will be case-specific and are certainly not a guaranteed safety net. Further, you may have reached agreement between you about only one or two aspects of your potential financial claims against each other, such as your house and maintenance, but in the absence of you having agreed about a savings account or a pension fund, you have not resolved the full extent of the financial issues and leave yourself open.

This is why getting legal advice is money well spent – it gives you the confidence and comfort of setting your expectations, assists you in the process of negotiating a settlement and makes sure that your settlement is correctly made legal.

CHAPTER 6

Court Proceedings

C OURT SHOULD ALWAYS be a last resort and you should still consider throughout the process whether you can bring the proceedings to an early end by any of the non-court dispute resolution options outlined in the previous chapter, which can all be instigated even once court proceedings have begun. They can run in parallel, so you can be engaging in mediation while awaiting a court hearing, and if you do not reach a settlement in mediation, you can then proceed with the court route.

You or your ex-partner will have to make a specific application to a court to start court proceedings. This will be on a specific form depending on what type of order you are asking a judge to make. A lawyer or a court advisor will be able to tell you which form to use for the application you want to make, and all of the court application forms are available online via the government's court forms website. At the time of writing, applications are made on paper and sent to the court by post, but the courts are trialling an online system in some locations with a view to enabling applications to be made online in the future.

Before you can make an application to court, except for an application for a divorce, in an emergency situation or where an exemption applies, you are required to attend a MIAM (see page 84). If you have started divorce proceedings you will not, by virtue of that process, also start proceedings to settle any issues about your children or finances. Each issue will have its own application form to start that process. Just because you need to start court proceedings for one issue (such as your financial settlement), it does not mean that you need to start court proceedings to deal with any other issues (such as your arrangements for your children). You are not required to be represented by a family lawyer to make an application to court. If you do not have a family lawyer acting on your behalf, you will be known as a 'litigant in person', although you can decide to later instruct a family lawyer during the process and become represented.

The court process varies depending on the issue in contention, but there are set procedures in place for each type of application. Making an application to court will mean that (apart from in a few emergency situations) your ex-partner will be sent a copy of your application form and know exactly what you have said and for which order you are applying. They will also get an opportunity to inform a judge of their views ahead of a first hearing, usually by completing a required court form and submitting it by a set date. The court will set a date for your first hearing, which is known as 'listing' a hearing, and notify you of that date and time. Unless you have a very good reason, such as being abroad on an unavoidable trip, or being unwell and having medical evidence from your doctor, you will be required to attend all court hearings with or without representation by a family lawyer.

Remember that at any point during court proceedings you can reach agreement with your ex-partner and bring your case to an end. If you are unable to settle your case yourselves then a judge will make a decision for you, and it is one that neither of you are likely to entirely agree with, so proceed with caution and remember the risk.

The Difference Between a Solicitor and a Barrister

Both solicitors and barristers can be referred to as 'lawyers', and those that practise family law can both be referred to as 'family lawyers', but both occupations have different roles in the legal process and you may not need both. A solicitor, if you instruct one:

- advises you and takes care of the running of your case on a day-to-day basis by communicating with you, your ex-partner or their family lawyer, the court, and any necessary third parties
- advises you on the remit of the law and applying it to your case
- outlines the strategy for resolving your dispute
- drafts your letters, documents (such as statements and financial disclosure) and consent orders

Barristers do not run your case on a day-to-day basis and instead are referred to as being 'at the coal face' – they are the ones who represent you in court and tell the judge in the court-room about your views on your case. Barristers will also draft the court orders made at court hearings.

Barristers are usually instructed ahead of a hearing for a meeting with you and your solicitor to give their specialist second opinion on strategy and settlement, and they will draft a Position Statement on your behalf ahead of each hearing, which sets out for a judge the background of your case and what your position is at that hearing, supported by reference to the law and with reference to the facts and evidence in your case. Your solicitor will usually shortlist some barristers for you who they think would be particularly good for your case, and decide with you which barrister to choose.

I am a solicitor, not a barrister. Clients usually find me through an online search, my firm's website, legal rankings, personal recommendations or Instagram. To instruct me people simply send me an email or pick up the phone. I am usually instructed by a client when they are thinking about separating or after their separation, and I advise them about their options and the legal process for how to anticipate and unravel any issues as a consequence of their separation. I advise and correspond with my client as and when they need me and, if they choose, I also correspond with their ex-partner/ their solicitor, the court and any other involved third parties, such as CAFCASS (see page 140). If there are court proceedings (and not all cases require court proceedings to resolve the disputes), I prepare my client's case for court as there are court required documents and information that must be completed in a set manner and done at particular times during the case. I instruct barristers to represent my clients at court, and can attend court with the barrister and my client to assist in furthering negotiations or make progress with the case while both sides of the case are at the court together. I work with the barrister in drafting the court orders or, if there have been no court proceedings, I will work with the ex-partner/their solicitor in drafting any settlement documents at the end.

Where there are complexities to a case or unusual circumstances it can be very useful for you and your solicitor to have a conference with a barrister early on in the process with a view to trying to reach an early settlement and avoid court, or with a view to carefully planning your case to make sure all the relevant evidence and any necessary experts are planned for from the beginning. Solicitors and barristers work together as a team for you. Solicitors can do advocacy in court (talking to the judge on your behalf), and some solicitors will do the day-to-day running of your case and also present your case to a judge in court, so you would not need a barrister to represent you at that hearing. It depends on the solicitor you instruct, how comfortable they are with advocacy, the complexities of your case, the complexity of each hearing or whether a second opinion would be of benefit in any event. It can also come down to cost.

Another difference between solicitors and barristers is that solicitors tend to charge on an hourly basis split into ten units. You are charged on a 'time spent' basis, so however long it takes your solicitor to undertake each task on your matter is charged in units of six minutes. Some solicitors do offer certain work on a fixed fee basis, for example the whole divorce will be completed for a sum fixed at the beginning of your case, regardless of how much time they spend doing that work. Barristers also have both options available to them but tend to fix their fees for specific tasks. For example, for a hearing listed to take one hour, they will give you a fixed fee for a specified amount of time which usually covers their prep-aration work, drafting of your position statement, corresponding with your solicitor, travelling to and from the hearing, and presenting your case at that hearing. It is only if your hearing goes on for much longer than estimated that they might then charge for any extra time on an hourly rate. This can work out more economical than a solicitor's 'time spent' charging basis. Barrister's fees are, however, agreed in advance of the hearing, usually about one week before, which means that whether or not your hearing goes ahead you must still pay them their fixed fee. This is because they will do their preparation work ahead of your hearing and will have blocked out time in their diary for your case.

However you fund your legal fees, your solicitor will usually ask for you to pay some money 'on account' which is paid into their firm's client account and held in advance of work they will undertake for you. Of course, should there be any money remaining on account at the conclusion of your instruction of your solicitor, your money will be transferred back to you. You should expect to receive a bill after any significant tasks are completed or, most commonly, on a monthly basis, for any work completed during that month. Your bill will be paid from that money you have already paid on account, and you will probably be asked to replenish it as appropriate. If there are any expenses to be paid on your behalf, such as a court fee, you will be asked to pay that amount to your solicitor's client account in advance of the expense being incurred. If you want a barrister, their fees will need to be paid in advance to your solicitor's client account too; the solicitor instructs the barrister on your behalf and is therefore liable for the barrister's fees. If you are one of the rare few that qualifies for Legal Aid, then your legally aided solicitor will talk you through your options within the remit of your legal aid funding to instruct a barrister for any court hearings you have, also covered by your legal aid funding.

Barristers will not communicate directly with you unless you are physically in their presence, either in a conference or at court with them. Your solicitor is responsible for instructing your barrister and providing them with the required information and will collaborate with them ahead of your hearing on your behalf. A solicitor is more able to concisely present your case to a barrister and discuss any complexities and legal issues, and works as a team with the barrister to best present and, hopefully, settle your case.

Some barristers do offer their services on a 'direct access' basis. This means that a litigant in person (someone who is not represented by a solicitor) can approach them to represent them at a court hearing without a solicitor in the middle. Not all barristers offer this and those who do will need to be satisfied that the litigant in person is capable of doing the work of the solicitor as they will not do it for you. If the litigant in person is not felt able to perform the requirements of a solicitor to the standards expected, a barrister will not be able to work with them, in which case you will need a solicitor's expertise and support.

Direct access is not to be confused with 'pro bono' work. Pro bono is rare and is where a solicitor or barrister might represent you without charge, sort of on a charitable basis. It is usually only for cases which have, for example, an interesting point of law that, if challenged through the courts, could produce new law.

Representing Yourself

A 'litigant in person' is the term for an individual who is representing themselves in court proceedings. It might be that you have taken legal advice in the run up to court proceedings being issued and feel able to represent yourself in the court process, or it might be that you cannot afford to instruct a solicitor to represent you in those proceedings.

Legal aid is no longer widely available, although it is worth checking your eligibility with a legal aid law firm if you think your circumstances might warrant it (see https://www.gov.uk/check-legal-aid).

Being represented in court proceedings means that your solicitor will perform all formal correspondence on your behalf, advise you throughout the process and manage your case in accordance with the court requirements and protocols. At court hearings, you will have someone in the courtroom speaking on your behalf, usually a barrister. In the absence of having a solicitor to represent you, the court and your spouse (if they are also a litigant in person) or their solicitor, and any other connected third parties, will correspond with you directly. You will be expected to progress your case and handle it to the same standard as a solicitor.

Most solicitors can be instructed to advise you without being formally on the court record as acting for you, which means that you have the benefit of legal advice in the background (throughout or at times when you feel it is most needed), but your spouse/their solicitors and the court are not obliged to communicate with them, which keeps your costs down. Barristers cannot be instructed by a litigant in person unless they offer their services on a direct access basis (see page 98).

In court proceedings, there will be hearings and you will need to present your case orally to a judge, in place of a barrister in court. If your hearing involves each party giving evidence, you will need to question your ex-partner on their evidence, which is usually a rather unpleasant experience for you both without a professional in between you. A litigant in person is allowed to be assisted in the day-to-day running of their case and in court at hearings by someone, usually a friend or family member, known as a 'McKenzie friend'. There are rules about what a McKenzie friend can and cannot do to assist a litigant in person, but generally they are there to take notes and talk through points with the litigant in person. They are not able to talk on behalf of the litigant in person, so they cannot talk to the judge or the other party in court proceedings. There is some helpful guidance about what McKenzie friends can do on the judiciary website: www.judiciary.uk/publications/mckenzie-friends/.

The reality is that you are unlikely to do as well as a trained and experienced family lawyer (solicitor or barrister) because, firstly, you do not have the years of specialist training and experience that the profession can offer and, secondly, because you are emotionally attached and this makes it harder for you to focus your case on your best legal points. You will be limited by your absence of that legal training and emotional detachment. I am aware that the reality for some is that paying for legal representation is not always possible. The judicial system is feeling the pressure as it has become increasingly populated by litigants in person, but remember that the standards expected of a litigant in person are the same as those expected of a professional. You will need to do your homework to understand what you have to do, when and in what format. The court staff cannot legally advise you, but they will signpost you in the direction of the right court form to use. The correspondence you receive from the court about your case will explain the next steps and tell you what you have to do and by when. It is not easy to be a litigant in person – try not to bury your head in the sand, leave dealing with requirements to the last minute or do a quick job in producing your documents. Each requirement should be considered as a 'one chance' event, so do it in a well-considered and thorough manner, whether that be with or without the assistance of a solicitor.

The Final Hearing

If you are unable to settle your case before a final hearing, a judge will make a binding decision on the outcome for you. It is rare for cases to go all the way to a final hearing – they usually settle by the parties reaching an agreement and submitting a consent order to the court before this last stage – and, in my experience, it's best to try to avoid one. The costs of your case going all the way to a final hearing should alone be enough to put you off allowing your case to go all that way. The other main reasons to settle before a final hearing are time, stress and emotion. It will take at least a year for your case to progress all the way to a final hearing, perhaps longer. The courts are inundated and tend to be under-resourced for the demand being placed upon them for hearings. A final hearing is the longest of the hearings; usually between one and three days, and sometimes more. For a judge to have a whole day or consecutive days available in their diary often means a long wait of many months. The delay means months of further uncertainty and interim arrangements that are probably unsuitable for one or both of you. By this time you have already undergone at least one, probably two or three, court hearings where the absence of settlement suggests your amicability and relationship with your ex-partner is poor at best, the emotional strain of which will no doubt be causing you anxiety and stress.

Proportionality (making sure the action taken or costs incurred are relevant to the end goal) is something that I discuss a lot with my clients throughout the progress of their dispute, and particularly so when court proceedings are started. This applies more so in financial cases then in children's matters, but the principle does still ring true for both types of dispute. In financial cases a judge will usually give the parties a stern warning about the proportionality of their inability to settle their dispute and the financial cost of them pursuing their case to a final hearing. It is commonly said that a person's costs are double again from the first and second stage hearings to go to the third final hearing. You must consider whether it is proportionate financially, in time, emotion and stress, for you to keep pursuing your case to a final hearing in the hope that a judge might favour your position in their final decision.

It's not just proportionality you should consider but also the inherent risk of litigation. You cannot choose your judge and, with all lawyers and judges, there are different opinions on what the right outcome should be, so you can never be sure that a judge will agree entirely with you. Even if a judge does make a favourable decision at the final hearing, there is then the potential for appeal and further delays and money to be spent. You can rid yourself of this uncertainty and risk by retaining autonomy over your outcome and reaching a settlement. A compromise will likely be necessary, but that will bring you back to the argument of proportionality and retaining control of your own outcome.

This is not to say that I haven't represented clients at final hearings. My job is to appraise my client of their chances of success and the range of outcomes, and it is their decision, not mine, to decide whether to litigate or settle. Sometimes it is out of their control – if their ex-partner is being unreasonable to the extent that what is on offer is too far beyond my client's realm for concession, then pushing forward with court and to a final hearing is necessary.

If you are contemplating pursuing a court application as a litigant in person, my advice is to proceed with caution. It is understandable why someone would need to undertake such a task without legal representation, because it's not affordable or due to the unavailability of legal aid, but it is in the absence of expert advice on not only the law, but also on strategy, settlement, proportionality and risk. To add to this is the risk that you could be ordered to pay your ex-partner's costs. The remit and likelihood of this happening differ depending on the type of case and how you have behaved in those proceedings, but it is a real and potentially very expensive risk of court. An order to pay your ex-partner's costs might be made during those proceedings, after one specific hearing or at the end in retrospect of their cost. This is possible when one of you has behaved very poorly or unreasonably within the proceedings, for example in failing to comply with a court order telling you to do something, such as providing your financial disclosure, or not doing something, which then causes the hearing to be rendered useless without that information.

Another consideration about paying your ex-partner's costs is if they don't have the same access to funds as you do in order to fund their representation in court. In some circumstances, they can apply to the court for a lump sum to be paid from you to them to pay their legal fees. Where you have to provide a lump sum, or have an order for their costs made against you, you could be responsible for all or a proportion of your ex-partner's costs for either a specific expense, a specific hearing or throughout the process. This certainly should be factored in when considering proportionality of pursuing court or making compromises to settle.

Likewise, if you are unable to get your ex-partner to reach an agreement with you and you do not have the funds to make an application to court, you should consider with a solicitor whether you could make an application against your ex-partner to give you funds to take matters to court. Telling your ex-partner about your ability to do this, or applying for a costs order against them if they unreasonably force your issues through the courts, might be the reminder of proportionality they need to deal with your dispute out of court.

CHAPTER 7

What to Do if Things Get Nasty

As MUCH AS you might hope for a Gwyneth Paltrow break-up of 'consciously uncoupling' or an Elvis Presley divorce of leaving the court holding hands with your now ex-spouse, the truth is that it is unlikely that you will achieve this (and, don't forget, they had PR people helping them!). What is likely is that you are both dealing with a lot of emotion and stress, and some people cope with that better than others. I would say that the majority of my clients are able to separate with civility and dignity, but sometimes relations between exes deteriorate to such an extent that it becomes an issue of its own that needs to be addressed. This chapter covers those types of situations and gives you some guidance on what to do if you are experiencing them.

Domestic Abuse

Domestic abuse is now acknowledged to cover a wide range of behaviours. Abuse is not just physical – it can be psychological, emotional and even monetary. A threat to hurt you or the act of hurting you, including a sexual act which hurts you, is physical abuse. Intimidation and harassment either from a partner, ex-partner or from one of their family members or friends encouraged by them, may also be abuse. Emotional abuse includes verbal insults and controlling behaviour, such as controlling what you do, what you wear, who you see and where you go. Abuse can extend to limiting you, isolating you from family or friends, or withholding money on purpose to prevent you from accessing food, clothes or services.

If you are experiencing abusive behaviour, you should try to get help as quickly as possible. I understand that this can sometimes be difficult. Concerns, such as not knowing if it is serious enough or whether you will be believed, or fear of your partner finding out, might be preventing you from taking action. However, just getting some advice about your options and talking to someone about it will be a step in the right direction.

There is a crossover between family law and criminal law in these situations. Family lawyers will not automatically become involved in any criminal proceedings, such as where the police have been called, are pressing charges or investigating your case. Police matters will be dealt with under criminal law. Family lawyers can become involved from a 'civil law' perspective and can assist alongside criminal proceedings, or in the absence of any police involvement or criminal proceedings.

A family lawyer will be able to discuss with you, confidentially, the abuse and what your options are under family law. Depending on the situation, the options will differ. Where genuine and significant harm is a risk, you should inform the police and make an application to court for an 'emergency protective order', and legal aid is sometimes available for these applications. This is used in a situation of domestic abuse that places you and/or your children in danger of significant harm. There is an exemption for domestic abuse situations which means that you are not required to attend a mediation MIAM before making an application to court, and you can quickly seek the protective orders you require. Urgent court applications can include orders to prevent the abuse continuing by preventing your ex-partner from contacting you, coming within a certain distance of you and from causing you any harm. This is known as a 'non-molestation order'. It extends to preventing them from encouraging others to communicate with you or cause you harm.

It is possible to ask a judge to give you a non-molestation order without telling your ex-partner that you are applying for it first, so they are unaware of your application, or it can be applied for having first told your ex-partner that you will be asking a judge for it. If a judge makes the non-molestation order your ex-partner needs to be personally served with the order, meaning someone needs to physically hand it to them. A process server is a person who will locate your ex-partner and personally serve them, even if it takes them a few attempts. You will need to provide information about the likely whereabouts of your ex-partner and what they look like. If they cannot be located or are not properly personally served, the order cannot be effective. This is important because, once served, breach of any of the terms will be a criminal offence. If it is breached such as by making contact with you, you can immediately call the police and the police can arrest them.

In addition to a non-molestation order, or sometimes as an alternative, you can apply to court for an 'occupation order', which removes your ex-partner from your shared home (rented or owned). The threshold for being successful in obtaining such an order is high as you are asking a judge to remove someone from their home, but if the risk of harm is significant enough to you and/or your children, the order can be made.

If you apply for either or both orders without first telling your ex-partner, and you are successful in convincing a judge that your situation is such that you require this type of protection, a judge will make the order for a short period first, usually for a week. At the same time the judge will arrange for another hearing to take place in about a week's time, and at that next hearing you and your ex-partner (and your respective family lawyers, if you have them) will both need to attend. The purpose of this second hearing is for the judge to hear the other side of the story. If you are served with a non-molestation order, occupation order, or both, this 'return hearing' is your opportunity to put your viewpoint forward, counter the allegations made against you (if appropriate) and see if you can agree a way forward. The return hearing is not to say that the judge did not believe the applicant at the first hearing, but fairness in law requires a judge to hear from you both. The judge can then decide whether to continue the order for a further set period of time, and that can continue to be extended in the future, if needed.

If you are served with one of these emergency protective orders you should immediately comply with the terms of the order(s) as it is immediately effective and the consequence of a breach is serious. Failing to keep to the restrictions placed upon you by the order(s), such as texting your ex-partner even if the order says you cannot communicate with them, means you could be arrested by the police. It is a criminal offence. You should take legal advice if you can, and most definitely make sure you attend the return hearing and have your voice heard, whether that be with or without legal representation.

For less urgent or harmful situations, there are non-urgent court options available at varying degrees of severity, and the best choice for you will depend on your situation – it is bespoke to you rather than a required process expected of you. If you choose not to apply for a court order, or if it is not felt that you would be successful in meeting the threshold required to successfully obtain one from a judge, a good option might be to get a family lawyer to write to your ex-partner on your behalf. It will be important for that letter to set out examples of their unacceptable behaviour and ask them to stop immediately, and the consequences of them failing to cease their behaviour will be set out in that letter, such as you then applying for a court order if they continue. It can include a request that your ex-partner gives you formal promises not to behave in specified ways and these can be the same as those specified in a non-molestation order. This type of 'warning letter' can be written at varying tones of severity appropriate to the situation.

Alternatives include making plans to remove yourself from a situation, such as moving out of your shared home. This can be done with the assistance of a family lawyer who can manage the communication of your move to your ex-partner, and attempt to limit any prejudice such a move might have against you. There are domestic abuse organisations that can assist you in moving out and into new accommodation, should you be in a situation of requiring an urgent place to live. If you are married then remember that you have financial claims against each other, and a letter from a family lawyer can also be sent setting out your monetary needs in addition to a warning letter, or an application to court can be made if financial arrangements are not swiftly agreed between you. My advice to remove yourself from the situation, which may mean your home, is really only when you feel there is no other option and you and/or your children are at risk of harm.

If the behaviour is ongoing you can opt for an urgent court order at any time. You do not need to worry that the option is removed if you do not apply immediately or if you are not initially successful at court. You can and should call the police at any time if you fear harm or you and/or your children are harmed. I always tell my clients that if anything happens their first call should be to the police and then they should contact me.

As this is a matter of one person causing harm to another, my advice differs somewhat to my usual 'be amicable' approach. Taking professional advice about what protection is best for you in your situation, which may evolve as your situation changes (it might change by the hour if something suddenly happens), is really the priority. You need to be aware of your options, and what the thresholds are for each option, and then you can make an informed decision about what is best for you. If you have children and you are in an abusive situation, remember to put your children first. I have given advice to many clients with children in domestic abuse situations of varying degrees and many have chosen to stay with their partner. That is a matter for them, but I do always tell them that there is a risk in that decision. You are expected to place your children's needs first and, if choosing to stay with an abusive partner places your children at risk of harm, it's vital to consider whether you are making the right choice for them. It may be that social services are informed of your situation (for example, from a school teacher or a concerned friend or neighbour), and they may question your ability to protect your children and can take their own protective action for them. Domestic abuse and its effect on your children, and on you as a parent, are taken into consideration when deciding the right arrangements for your children post-separation (see Chapter 9 for more on this).

Child Abduction

Whatever your relationship status with your children's other parent, if you have genuine reason to believe that they might take your children out of England and Wales without your permission or not return them as agreed, you should take urgent advice from a family lawyer. To remove a child without consent or retain them for longer than permitted outside of England and Wales is child abduction, which is a criminal offence.

If you fear that this might happen, there are urgent steps you can take to try to prevent it. Practically, you should locate your children's passport(s) and any other travel documentation and move those documents to a safe location, such as a friend or family member's home, or even your family lawyer's office. You can notify the passport office or another country's embassy if your children might be eligible for a passport from another country, to inform them that you do not consent to another passport or travel document being produced for your children. This is not in itself binding, but it might help.

With the assistance of the police (and usually a family lawyer), you can trigger a 'Port Alert' which informs all national ports, to include airports and ferry ports, of your children's details and the risk that they might be imminently abducted so they can assist in preventing your children's travel if they are seen at a port.

You can make an application to court for a court order preventing your ex-partner from removing your children from England and Wales. The application would be for a 'Prohibitive Steps Order' if you apply before they have gone, or there are 'Location Orders' if they have already been moved. This should be done in conjunction with taking preventative steps with your children's travel documents and triggering a port alert, and you will need to explain why it is you do not agree that your children should be taken abroad by your ex-partner, what risk you believe such travel poses to your children's welfare and why safeguards could not be put in place to enable that travel to happen.

It may be that travel abroad could be made possible by seeking an order from the court which includes safeguards. The purpose of a safeguard is to keep the travelling parent to their word about their travel plans and can include penalties if they do not. Safeguards can provide the 'left behind' parent with legal assurances and provision to enable them to act should the conditions of their children's travel not be kept to by the other parent. The country of destination is likely to make a difference to the risk factor of your children travelling there. There are many countries that have signed up to reciprocal agreements which makes it easier for children to be returned from that country if they are wrongly taken there or retained there.

There are other countries that do not have such agreements with England and Wales and they are therefore risker to travel to with children. Safeguards can be set out as conditions in a court order allowing your children to be removed to another country for a specified period (whether it be for a holiday or a prolonged period) and can include obtaining a mirror order in the destination country, which means that the terms of the order made in England are made again in the destination country's court. This makes sure that those terms are then enforceable in the destination country, as they have been made under their local laws. Alternatives include obtaining undertakings (enforceable promises to the court) about commitment to the conditions of the children's travel to the other country, such as facilitating the children's contact with the 'left behind' parent, a payment of money if they breach the conditions and payment of the 'left behind' parent's legal fees should future court proceedings be required due to any breaches. This is a complex area of law and any such issues will need to be carefully considered and crafted bearing in mind your specific situation.

On the assumption that your children are accepted as residing in England and Wales (and this is an important legal issue to be discussed with a family lawyer), if your children are taken abroad without your consent, or if they have been taken abroad with your consent but then kept abroad against your agreement, you will need to act quickly and take professional advice. This is child abduction. You will need to make sure that you have not given your consent or that the other parent has not misunderstood somehow that you did give your consent. You should immediately contact the police and provide them with as much detail about your children, the person or people you believe them to have travelled with, any of the travel details you might know (from where, when and how, and to where and when), and provide any court orders or documents you have which relate to the incident, such as text messages or emails with your ex-partner. The priority will be to locate your children and have them returned to England and Wales, and you should immediately instruct a family lawyer who can make an application to the courts here to do just that. Once the children are returned, the courts can then unravel what has happened and decide where your children should be (here or another country), and that country's courts (either here or there) can decide what the arrangements will be for your children going forward in light of this incident.

Social Media

Our lives are increasingly visible online, and social media and group messaging have become part of our everyday lives. This makes it very easy for people to air their issues publically or behave in a way online in which they would not ordinarily do in person. When tensions and emotions run high it is very tempting to type in anger and, because you are not saying it directly to a person, it feels far more accessible and easy to do. The consequences, however, can be much worse.

No matter how badly someone has behaved, I urge you not to write anything about it on social media or in messages. You are committing your views to writing, possibly also to public viewing, and this is very hard to erase. If you post a comment, as cryptic as you think it might be, the point is you are doing it because you want to communicate your feelings to someone out there. Even if you think you are the one in the right, you are lowering your moral high ground by displaying your discontent or exposing your ex-partner's wrongdoings for all to see. In the heat of the moment, or even after consideration, it will not be good. Even if you delete the post afterwards, someone could have saved it or taken a screenshot and its distribution is then no longer under your control.

Negative posts can attract others' comments and the risk of a public argument. You do not want to get into a dispute with your ex-partner or their family or friends on social media for all to see. The drama, the public embarrassment, the dividing of sides and the legacy that remains are very hard to come back from and repair to an amicable status.

#Blessed

Just as negative posts can come back to haunt you, positive posts may have a similar effect. You might have posted photos of you and your then-partner happily together or posted a complimentary Father's/Mother's Day photo of them with your children with a lovely comment or hashtag, but then in a later fallout seek to rely on historical behaviours as either an example of their unreasonable behaviour or limited parenting ability. Your ex-partner could use your previous posts as evidence to contradict you. It is widely accepted that the grids of Instagram are not a true reflection of what goes on behind closed doors, so they are not in themselves proof of the truth, but do be conscious about the timing and content of your personal posts.

Be mindful of how your standard of lifestyle is documented online during your marriage and post-separation. If in your financial negotiations on divorce you try to downplay your standard of living in an attempt to limit your spouse's claims against you by saying that their stated needs are not aligned with the marital standard of living, it might be easily countered by your own online posts showing holidays, nice cars or jewellery, for example. Discovery of new relationships and even cohabitation might be proved by your own or your new partner's online posts. I've even used a new partner's TripAdvisor reviews to evidence my client's ex-spouse's jet-set lifestyle in contradiction to how he portrayed it within court proceedings.

One of the first things ex-partners do after an argument or split is to block each other or start online deleting. If you think any of their previous posts or messages to you or a third party, negative or positive, might be useful for you to have in the future, I recommend screenshotting them before you are blocked or they are deleted. Save them somewhere safe and send them on to a trusted friend or family member or, even better, to your family lawyer for safekeeping. It may be that they form part of your evidence should your dispute require it in the future.

Smart Devices and Unsmart Decisions

Most people have smart devices which are used to manage their lives, communicate with others and store documents and photos. Devices are commonly synced with each other, such as your phone being synced with a tablet or laptop or another person's phone. Family sharing is actively encouraged by phone companies, such as family sharing of virtual photo albums and calendars. Your phone might not just sync photos with your tablet or laptop but your location, phone records, messages and emails are also likely to sync, meaning that they are visible and accessible on those other devices too. It is important that you are aware of what personal information on your phone goes elsewhere and to whom it is visible, and make swift changes if you are not happy with it.

For example, I advocate people taking advice from a family lawyer if they are considering whether to separate from their partner without telling their partner they are taking advice. You might make an appointment and place it in your calendar, and when attending the appointment your location might be picked up by your device. You may not have thought about whether your calendar appointment automatically syncs with your partner's phone or another device which is accessible by them, and you may have inadvertently just informed them of your meeting. In some domestic abuse situations, partners often use phone location services to keep track of their partner and the location of a family lawyer's office is unlikely to go down well. Before or after your meeting, your lawyer might email you, and your emails may pop up on another device and be readable by your partner.

If you share devices at home, such as a tablet or laptop that you both access, be mindful about accessing your partner's or ex-partner's personal accounts without their permission. It should go without saying, but do not login to their accounts or access their personal information without consent. If they have left their account logged in on a shared device, you should not treat it as an invitation to snoop, as tempting as it may be. If their phone is unlocked that does not mean you can take a scroll through their messages or social media accounts. Even though you have not had to type in their password, you are still hacking as you are accessing their personal accounts without express consent. Likewise, if they have done it to you, it does not give you the green light to do it to them. If it feels wrong then it probably is wrong, and it is a crime which can mean the police getting involved.

The rules on snooping extend beyond computers and are strict. You cannot snoop through another person's personal paperwork, files or belongings, even if they are your partner's or ex-partner's. You are not allowed to take copies of your ex-partner's personal documents without their consent. Your family lawyer will not be able to look at any documents or copies of any documents you have unless they are jointly addressed to you or your ex-partner has given them to you. If your ex-partner leaves out a document in a communal area or shared room and you happen to see it, you are allowed to write down your own note and inform your lawyer about what you remember seeing. Ideally, I recommend keeping a file (well away from your spouse), to include this information along with your own diary of events and printed out records of messages, screenshots or notes about what's been said, by whom and when.

When communicating with your ex-partner it is important to apply ordinary social boundaries to that communication. In the heat of an argument it is not uncommon for offensive words to be used, or for multiple messages to be sent or multiple attempts to call the other to be made. I have often been told by clients that in a dispute over arrangements for the children, for example, such as waiting outside a house to collect the children only to be refused, or when attempting to have a pre-arranged telephone call with your children but it not being answered or denied, they have sent multiple messages or made numerous attempts to call. Of course, this behaviour is not limited to those with children. In these examples, the person sending messages or making the calls feels that they are the wronged person and they are entitled to seek contact and make those multiple attempts to communicate that message to their ex-partner. However, if your ex-partner tells you to stop with your repeated attempts and you continue anyway, you might find yourself in trouble with the police. It can be a criminal offence to misuse communications or harass someone in this way. If your ex-partner has not kept to their side of the agreement, avoid bombarding them and apply normal social boundaries to how you communicate with them about the issue. If your dispute is not resolved then work through my advice in Chapter 4 about successfully communicating with your ex-partner.

Not only do our mobile devices double-up as telephones, cameras and calendars, many also offer recording facilities. It is very easy to record a phone call or conversation with someone by the quick press of a button on your phone. A step up from this is easily available video cameras, tracking devices and spy software. Just as I said before, if it feels wrong it probably is wrong. You cannot record someone, including your own children, whether that be an audio or video recording, watch or listen to someone, track their whereabouts or use computer software to monitor them, without their consent and knowledge. To present evidence about your case obtained via an unauthorised or illegal method does not paint you in a good light and is frowned upon.

I am very conscious of these modern hurdles with my clients and advise them about turning off their location services, switching off phones entirely during meetings, being wary of synced devices, changing passwords and setting up entirely new and private email accounts from which they can confidentially communicate with me. Where appropriate, I have used encrypted services for phone calls and exchanging messages with clients, planned for calls at times, locations and on numbers unknown to their ex-partner, and even set up new email accounts for my clients. I am finding these modern technology issues increasingly common and, with that, police involvement is becoming more common in cases. Avoid temptation and remove your ex-partner's temptation by unsyncing, changing passwords, blocking and setting up new accounts where necessary.

PART IV

CHILDREN AND CO-PARENTING

CHAPTER 8

Initial Considerations

A LTHOUGH YOU AND your partner have agreed to separate, you have children and that will forever tie you together. Co-parenting post-separation will be different for each family as your children and your situation are unique to you. The law states that your children are the primary concern and their best interests are 'paramount', but what this means for you is up to you as parents to decide. I have set out some guidance on this in this chapter, but remember that there is no set formula. You and your ex are likely to disagree about how to interpret what is in your children's best interests, and so you should prepare yourself for some compromise. It is going to feature heavily in your future as co-parents, and is the best grounding to the success of that new relationship.

How to Tell Your Children

H ow to tell your children is often one of the first considerations of couples upon separation and it is also so often a cause of dispute, where one partner tells the children without the other being present or, worse, without the other's knowledge. I always suggest that as parents you should agree with each other first about what you will say to the children, and then jointly sit down with them all together to communicate the same message. Children do not need to know what the cause of the breakdown is; they do not need to know if one of their parents has behaved badly or if another person was involved; and they do not need to have either parent pinpointed as the one to blame. Relate offers some very useful guidance and tips on how to tell your children, particularly for different age groups, and I recommend taking a look at https://www.relate.org.uk/relationship-help/help-separation-and-divorce/talking-about-separation/telling-children for more advice.

If it is part of your initial plan that you will continue to live separately under the same roof, then you may not need to tell your children anything until the time comes when one of you moves out. Your children will need to be very young (babies and toddlers) for this to be appropriate. If your children are of an age where they will be aware that their parents are sleeping in different rooms, an explanation will need to be given. If your separation is temporary while you try to reconcile then carefully consider what it is that you tell them. It may be best not to disclose any relationship difficulties and instead find lighter, easy to understand (and therefore accept without question) excuses.

Where possible, the message should be given jointly. Explain to your children that you have decided to separate but that you both love them very much, that they are not to blame and that they will continue to spend time with you both. If you have already reached an agreement about what the arrangements will be for the children, either just for the immediate future or long-term, then you can explain those arrangements to them, if it is age-appropriate. If you are in any doubt about how to approach this, bearing in mind your own children's individual needs and understanding, I would recommend (jointly, if possible) seeking professional guidance and your family lawyer should be able to put you in touch with the right person, such as a family therapist or your child's GP who can offer more bespoke signposting for your children.

Unfortunately, it happens a lot where one parent tells the children without the other parent's prior consultation or presence. This then infuriates the other parent, and a conflict ensues. The children's best interests must always be placed front and centre of your considerations at this time, and a joined-up approach from both parents will be the best way to communicate the news, no matter how you feel towards your (ex-)partner.

How you tell your children is not only very important to their own welfare and understanding, it is also important for your future co-parenting relationship and, possibly, future court proceedings. If you start with a united co-parenting front it helps to put the right foundations in place for co-parenting going forward. If you don't and you go on to disagree over the arrangements for your children to the extent that a judge is required to resolve your dispute for you, then how you dealt with this may be brought into those court proceedings. It is likely to be used as an example of how you did not deal with an issue regarding the children with their best interests at the forefront, so be conscious about the lasting effect, not only on your children's emotional welfare but also on any future court proceedings.

It is advisable to discuss any change in your home life with your children's teacher(s) or other significant adults in their lives, such as a treating doctor, if appropriate. Informing them, on a confidential basis, of the potential for the issues at home or news of your separation to impact upon your children allows them to be mindful of your children's needs, and any new behaviours they might display. It is important to try to do this as a joint discussion, but if that is not possible, don't rely on your now ex-partner to do it or to feedback to you any information they receive in response. You should engage jointly and independently to make sure you are giving your opinion and receiving any messages in return from the horse's mouth.

Parental Responsibility

Parental responsibility is a term I have seen on forms, such as some medical documents and even a registration for a nursery, but I think it is a term that is little understood by parents. After giving birth, the mother (and father if present) is given information about parental responsibility as part of the birth registration pack, but I very much doubt parents of a newborn remember the legal terminology later on, or if an already separated father of that newborn is given the same information.

Parental responsibility is important to understand from the moment you start to think there are issues in your relationship. What happens naturally or through common sense when your relationship is working might suddenly or slowly grind to a halt and a parent could find themselves as an 'outsider' to their children's lives by virtue of their relationship breakdown.

Parental responsibility is the right to be consulted about and take part in all the big decisions about your children's lives, which include decisions about their health, education, where they live, religious upbringing, their finances and their name.

When you are together it might go without saying that you talk about any such big decisions, for example whether your child should have an operation, but when separated you might find that you are no longer automatically consulted as part of that decision process.

Another common example of a parental responsibility issue post-separation is in respect of your children's religious upbringing. While a couple who are of different faiths may be able to overcome their differences when they are happily together, often their religious differences can become more fraught when children are involved, whether that be from themselves, family pressure or tradition. Making decisions such as whether to have a child baptised should be a decision that both parents discuss together. Where parents cannot agree over such a parental responsibility issue they will need a judge to make the decision for them.

There is a threshold for the level at which a decision about your children is a 'parental responsibility decision' and a day-to-day decision that would not require consultation between parents. Decisions such as taking your child to the doctor about an earache would not necessarily meet the threshold of requiring consultation with the other parent, but consent for an operation for grommets would require consultation. For all of the big parental responsibility decisions in a child's life, you must consult with each other and try to agree the decision. You should try to agree between yourselves, but if you can't agree then follow the advice on using non-court resolution options in Chapter 5 and, if they do not work, you will need to make an application to court.

A child's mother (birth or adoptive) automatically has parental responsibility for that child. If the child's father is married to the mother at birth, the father will also automatically have parental responsibility, or will later acquire it by subsequently marrying the mother. For fathers who are unmarried and have children born after 1 December 2003, they will have parental responsibility for them if they are named on the birth certificate as the father. If a biological father does not have parental responsibility by virtue of any of the above options, he can ask the mother to enter into a parental responsibility agreement with him. This is a straightforward form that must be formally signed and witnessed and sent to the court for it to be effective. You can download a copy of this form (Form C(PRA1)) from the government website (https://www.gov.uk/government/publications/form-cpra1-parental-responsibility-agreement).

A step-parent can also ask to enter into a parental responsibility agreement so that they too acquire parental responsibility for their stepchildren. In a separated family where both birth or adoptive parents have parental responsibility a step-parent would need both parents to agree and enter into the parental responsibility agreement with them. This is usually a practical solution for a situation where a step-parent is involved in the day-to-day care of the children, for example, taking them to medical appointments and therefore needing to be able to consent to treatment. For all parental responsibility decisions, everyone with parental responsibility, for example, both birth parents and a step-parent, must be consulted, so the more people who have it the more people that need consulting and have a say. In an acrimonious situation it may be difficult to obtain agreement for a step-parent to acquire parental responsibility. In that situation, it will be a matter of deciding how important it is to your family for a step-parent to acquire those rights balanced against the potential worsening of tensions between parents.

Anyone else with existing parental responsibility for the child would need to agree and sign the form. For parents and step-parents alike, having parental responsibility or not having parental responsibility has no effect on the financial responsibility for a child. The requirement to pay child maintenance is not dependent on whether a parent has parental responsibility for the child. For a step-parent this means that they can partake in the major decisions concerning their stepchildren without overriding the birth parent's requirement to pay child maintenance.

I have had pregnant clients ask me whether they should name the biological father on the birth certificate having separated from them. My advice applies to this situation and any other situation where a father has not acquired parental responsibility, and that is that as long as there is no dispute over the paternity of the child, it should not be withheld. If a mother unreasonably refuses to agree to the father obtaining parental responsibility, he will be left with no option but to apply to court for a parental responsibility order, which will be granted by a judge if there is no paternity dispute nor extreme welfare concerns for the child or mother.

CHAPTER 9

How to Decide the Right
Arrangements for Your Children

I UNDERSTAND THAT THE most important consideration for any parent post-separation is deciding how their children should spend their time. The fear of not knowing what the arrangements will be for your children, and whether they will live with you or when you will get to spend time with them, can be all-encompassing. There is no set formula in law to tell you how to resolve this – it is all case-specific, meaning that it depends entirely on your family situation. What happened to your friend or relative may not be right for your family, so be careful not to make assumptions based on what you have seen happen to others. There are no set presumptions in law that a mother has more say than a father, so do not prejudice yourself with any misleading preconceptions of the law.

The law and your family are the guiders here. There are many different terms used under the umbrella of 'arrangements for children'. You might have heard of the American phrase of 'custody' and the previously used English terms of 'residence' and 'contact'. These terms all tend to refer to what is now termed 'child arrangements' and the law says that if you apply to the court for an order that says anything about with 'whom a child is to live, spend time or otherwise have contact with, and when a child is to live, spend time or otherwise have contact with any person' this is all referred to under the umbrella term of 'child arrangements'. The terms 'custody' and 'residence' are not used due to the inference that the parent 'with residence' had greater rights over the child than the parent who 'had contact' with the child.

Throughout this book I will make reference to 'arrangements for your child' and by this I mean who your children stay with overnight and when your children spend time with each parent. When discussing arrangements with your ex-partner, you, too, should be conscious about the terminology and language you are using. In law, a court order that says that children 'live with' both parents can mean anything from an equal division of the children's time with both parents, and also an unequal arrangement where, for example, the children live with one parent 13 nights out of 14 and live with the other parent one night out of those 14. The unequal arrangement does not detract from the fact that the children 'live with' both parents. Not all orders will say that children live with both parents, but they are increasingly common as both parents are given the same status on the order which acknowledges them as having equal importance in their children's lives, even if their time is spent unequally between them.

Using old or American phrasing is likely to cause friction in your direct discussions with your ex-partner if the phrasing is used in such a way that it makes them feel like a lesser parent. Being conscious about your terminology and not using any words to make your ex-partner feel pushed out of your children's lives, even if the reality is that they physically see them less often than you, shows that you respect them as an equal parent and hopefully sets a standard of mutual respect and reassurance of each other's rights and responsibilities as co-parents.

Your children's best interests are the priority in law, and as parents you are expected to be able to make decisions for your children with their best interests in mind, and therefore the court is not automatically involved in deciding the arrangements for your children upon separation. It is presumed that it is in your children's best interests for them to have a relationship with both of their parents. Of course, this can be rebutted if there are circumstances which mean it would not be the case, such as the children's safety and welfare being put at significant risk by a relationship with a parent. However, this is only in extreme situations.

For the majority, it will be appropriate for your children to have a relationship with both of their parents, and it is a matter of deciding the logistics of how those ongoing relationships can be facilitated now that the family has two homes. Even though you are separated, you are still a family and you will continue to be a family for many years to come. I think it's important to keep that in mind and remember that for all those future major life events, such as big birthdays, graduations, weddings, grandchildren, you will both still be their parents and the ideal situation is that you will both be able to attend and be civil with each other.

The different types of arrangements for your children

There are different types of arrangements to facilitate your children's ongoing relationship with both of you now that you are separated. One arrangement is 'direct contact' which is where your children are physically with you and in your care. This can include 'overnight contact' where the children stay with you overnight. When your children are not in direct contact with you, you can consider 'indirect contact', which can be anything from telephone calls and video calls where you have 'live contact' with your children over a phone, to text messages or emails and sending letters/cards/gifts in the post. It's quite usual to agree arrangements for children to include both direct and indirect types of contact. In an ideal situation, you will be able to agree that your children spend time with both parents to include direct, overnight and indirect contact. It does not have to be one or the other.

In my experience, disputes between parents about arrangements for their children are usually borne out of them each wanting to spend more time with the children than the other is willing to agree. On the flip side, I have had clients complain that they want their ex-partner to spend more time with their children but they aren't willing to. In this situation it is very difficult because you cannot force a parent to spend time with their children, and when you think about it, would it really be in your children's best interests to do so if you know your ex-partner does not want to be there?

Many people think that children automatically stay with the mother, while the father gets to see them on alternate weekends. This is not true. There are many factors that get taken into account when deciding what the arrangements should be, such as any health issues or special needs of the children, the historical pattern of care, logistics and, to some extent, the children's own wishes and feelings. It is a balancing exercise of all those factors that will determine what arrangement could work for your family. It is unlikely that both parents will be happy with the outcome, but it is important to be reasonable and put your children's needs at the forefront of your mind when discussing the arrangements.

Where siblings are involved it may not be assumed that each child's best interests are the same. Factors such as differences in age, stages of development and personal needs will need to be weighed in the balance. However, it is unusual for siblings to be treated differently and it is better (where possible and appropriate) for the arrangements to apply to all the children so that they are kept together.

If you have concerns about abuse or your children's welfare while with one parent, you should take advice from a family lawyer to decide what level of safeguards might be appropriate. There can be additional safeguards put in place to direct contact, but these are only used in a situation where there is a genuine welfare concern for the children being alone with that parent. A safeguard is put in place to help to alleviate those concerns, rather than the concerns preventing the contact from taking place at all. There is the rare situation where it might be decided that it is in the children's best interests that they have no contact with a parent at all. You will need family law advice if you think this might apply to your children.

Just as with other family law disputes, you can resolve your child arrangements by discussions between the two of you, via mediation, solicitors' correspondence, arbitration or (as a last resort) court.

CONTACT CENTRES

The most protective safeguard for direct contact is for it to take place in a contact centre. A contact centre is often used in situations where there has been abuse or allegations of abuse sufficient to warrant safeguards for a child and sometimes also for a parent. The parents can be kept separated and safe and the contact worker moves the child between rooms to avoid the parents seeing each other. Siblings can attend together, but it will depend on your children's ages and specific circumstances whether this is appropriate for them.

Contact centres are not for use in the long-term, as it is hoped that they can be used alongside other measures, such as a parenting programme or domestic abuse work, as a stepping stone to the contact progressing at some point in the future away from the contact centre. The use of a contact centre may come with a cost, and you may have to pay for the facility, depending on the centre's own charging rates and your afford-ability (some may offer lower charging rates or, if you have it, your legal aid funding may cover the fee). It is possible for you to agree that one parent should pay the cost of the contact centre sessions – it does not always have to be equally shared. There might be logistical issues for you to consider, such as which contact centre to choose to suit both parents and how you will each get there. This option also comes with a delay as contact centres are in high demand and you may need to go on a waiting list before the contact can take place.

A contact centre tends to offer two differing levels for safe-guarding contact. The first is 'supervised' contact, where the contact between the parent and child is arranged for a specific time, date and period, and is supervised at all times by a 'contact supervisor' who closely monitors the contact by being with you, interacting with you and your child (such as encour-aging or making suggestions), and taking notes. These notes can then be used as evidence in related court proceedings about the arrangements for your child to feed back to the judge on how the relationship is developing. The second level is 'supported contact' in the contact centre where the parent and child are together in a room with other parents who are also doing the same thing, and there is a contact supervisor in the room as a protective measure, but not sat with you specifically. They will not produce notes about your contact session.

Intermediaries

If you do not want to use a contact centre, or a contact centre is not appropriate but you would like a safeguard to be put in place, it could instead be agreed that a family member or mutual friend should be present during the child's direct contact with a parent. This safeguard will need to be justified and is usually agreed as a way of avoiding a contact centre. It is quite a big ask of a family member or friend so bear in mind the burden on them and know that it is only likely to be possible as a temporary arrangement. The terminology used when agreeing to have a family member or friend present can be important. Make sure that you distinguish whether you are agreeing to 'supervision' by that person, in which case they need to be engaging with the parent and child at all times, or whether you are agreeing to the child's time with that parent being 'supported' by that person, in which case they will be with them but more in the background and there in case of need.

What the Law Says

The law is very clear that in any dispute about how to raise a child, that child's welfare is paramount, meaning that the child's best interests come first. Working out how to achieve what is in the child's best interests within individual family situations is difficult because the needs of a child vary so much from one family to the next. There are therefore no set rules about where and when a child should spend time with each parent. The law is discretionary and takes into account multiple factors which will be finely balanced in different proportions in different cases. In all children's cases which go to court a judge must consider the child's best interests by reference to what is called the 'Welfare Checklist'. It is useful for all parents who disagree over what is in their children's best interests, even if their dispute it not in court, to understand what a judge would consider if they were involved in their dispute so the right concerns are taken into account.

The Welfare Checklist is set out in written law, specifically The Children Act 1989, from which judges are given the boundaries of how they should approach and consider disputes about a child's upbringing. You may have heard reference to 'case law' which means laws that have come to fruition after other people's cases have been disputed through the courts. The decisions made in those cases, specifically how The Children Act was applied and the judge's decisions, then also become law and give guidance about how The Children Act can be interpreted and applied in different situations. It is from both The Children Act and case law that decisions are made by judges and from where a family lawyer will provide you with bespoke advice. The main points of the Welfare Checklist for you to bear in mind as a parent are as follows:

1. the ascertainable wishes and feelings of your child (considered in the light of your child's age and understanding)
2. your child's physical, emotional and educational needs

3. the likely effect on your child of any change in his circumstances
4. your child's age, sex, background and any characteristics which the court considers relevant
5. any harm which your child has suffered or is at risk of suffering and
6. how capable each parent, and any other person who is relevant, is of meeting your child's needs.

By the time clients come to me they have usually already had discussions with their ex-partner about the arrangements for their children, or they have at least thought about what they would want those arrangements to be. Without any knowledge of or reference to the law, all of my clients have considered many of the points on the Welfare Checklist, purely out of common sense. However, there is a spectrum of how different people will interpret what is best for the children's welfare, and this can lead to disputes. The fact that your relationship has broken down to the point that you cannot reach an agreement shows that you and your ex-partner have different views and place importance on or prioritise matters differently. This does not necessarily mean that either or both of you are being unreasonable. Your best-case scenario and your ex-partner's best-case scenario mark the boundaries within which the outcome of your dispute lies. By way of (a polarised) example, if your dispute relates to who your children should live with and when, and you think your children should live with you, and your ex-partner thinks they should live with them, the answer lies in either one of those options, or anywhere in between.

There is no set formula or framework to answer those questions starting with who, what and when, but the Welfare

Checklist is the law's answer to the 'why' question. You and your ex-partner will no doubt have different answers when considering your children's best interests. Disputes arise over how passionately you each believe your answer to be correct and therefore how much impact you believe compromising your views will have on your children's welfare.

Your Children's Wishes and Feelings

Depending on your relationship with your ex-partner, your family dynamics and parenting opinions, you might both agree on what you think your children's views are likely to be and incorporate those into your arrangements post-separation. However, more commonly, you both disagree on what you think your children will want and therefore (depending on your children's age and understanding) you might need to obtain their opinions.

Your children's views can be considered as part of deciding the plan of care for them now that you are separated. There is no hard and fast rule about this, but the general feeling is that the older and more mature the child is, the more weight their views will carry. Their views will need to be considered in the balance with the rest of the Welfare Checklist points, so they are not in themselves conclusive.

You should be very careful about obtaining your children's views independent of the other parent, if at all. Children, at any age, can be manipulated into airing a view which prefer-ences the questioning parent. Your children may even give conflicting opinions, finding themselves between their parents and giving sympathetic answers to each parent because that is what they think that parent wants to hear and they want to please them. Informing the other parent of independently taken opinions will, of course, cause upset and attract criticism for having such a discussion with your children in isolation of the other parent. The best-case scenario is that you and your ex-partner are able to agree the arrangements without the need to engage your children in the discussions.

CAFCASS

Where there are court proceedings about the arrangements for your children, your children's views can be taken as part of those proceedings. A child aged six or seven is at the younger end of the spectrum for their views to be considered and, even then, their views will not carry as much weight as an older child's. Older teenagers tend to formulate their own opinion about who they want to spend time with and when. In a situation where they get on well with both parents, convenience to their life as they know it will be a priority to them. Their views about who they should live with and when will likely prioritise the parent whose location (and possibly parenting style) enables them to continue with their day-to-day activities, seeing their friends, partaking in their hobbies and attending their school or college. Older teenagers will start to vote with their feet on plans that you make for them and their views will therefore carry more weight, but even this has to be carefully managed and is not the end answer just because your teenager says they do not agree. Despite your best parenting intentions, if your agreed arrangements for them post-separation means, for example, that they miss out on social activities they had previously enjoyed, their older age and increased independence (compared to a younger child) can mean that they simply do as they please anyway.

This is why older teenagers will need careful management if their own views conflict with your own and/or your ex-partner's.

It is easy to get into a scenario where a child gives a strong view against spending as much or any time with one parent and the parent 'with care' of that child simply says 'I can't make them go'. However, instead of using your children's views as a trump card to end the discussion about arrangements, attention should be given as to why they have that strong view, and what might be done to encourage them to spend more time with the other parent. Remember that for the majority of cases, the best interests of a child's welfare are to have a relationship with both parents, regardless of how you feel towards your ex-partner. Where there is an issue about a child's relationship with a parent it needs investigation, help and encouragement, not a closed door. This is why a child's view alone might not trump the other factors on the Welfare Checklist.

If court proceedings are started by either you or your ex-partner, the court will give a copy of the application form to an advisor from the Children and Family Court Advisory and Support Service (CAFCASS). CAFCASS is made up of the court's own advisors who are involved automatically in every court case relating to a child. An advisor will be allocated to your case ahead of the first court hearing and that advisor is tasked with understanding the issues in dispute, taking opinions on board and making recommendations to a judge about how best to resolve the disputes.

Before the first court hearing the CAFCASS advisor will contact each parent over the telephone and take a note of each parent's view of the issues in dispute. The CAFCASS worker will also do background checks with the police and social services for any involvement with either parent or child. From these brief telephone calls and the background checks, the CAFCASS worker will prepare a Safeguarding Letter to the judge ahead of the hearing and copies of it will be given to both parents, usually a couple of days before the hearing, or at court on the day of the hearing. The CAFCASS worker will set out in that letter the discussions they had with each parent to highlight to the judge the issues in dispute and both parents' views on those issues. They will then set out their initial advice to the judge about what is required to progress the case and narrow the gap between the parents.

The CAFCASS worker will only have limited initial information and so their advice should not be considered as a pre-determination of your case. For example, if your dispute is about who your children should live with and how much time they should spend with each parent, the CAFCASS worker is likely to be asked to give their view on the interim arrangements for your children between that court hearing and the next, and, if age-appropriate, prepare what is known as a Section 7 Report or a 'Wishes and Feelings' Report. Section 7 of The Children Act 1989 says that a judge can ask a CAFCASS worker to prepare a report on 'the matters which relate to the welfare of the child'. This means that in each case a judge will need to decide, with the views of the parents considered, what issues the report should consider as important to determining the welfare of your children. Each case will be different and the discretion of our laws means that the progress of each case is bespoke to your children and the specific issues in dispute.

If it is appropriate to your child's age (usually around aged 6–7 years and older) and level of understanding, the CAFCASS worker will meet with your child as part of their research in preparing their Section 7 Report. Your child will speak with the CAFCASS worker alone (unsupervised) and independently of either parent or sibling. This usually takes place at their school or, if that is not possible, some other location away from either of your homes. Your child will be asked in an appropriate, neutral and careful manner how they feel about the issue, for example, if the issue is spending time with each parent. They will not be asked outright who they want to live with, and neither parent should say anything like that to them either as it is not appropriate to place the burden of that decision on a child.

Your child's views will also be ascertained by the CAFCASS worker through discussions they will have with both parents (separately), and sometimes also your child's teacher. In some situations, speaking to wider family members or other important people in your child's life can also be done. Your wishes and feelings, your child's teacher's understanding and opinion and, if appropriate, other family member's interpretations, all form part of the CAFCASS worker's research and will be considered when making their recommendations to the judge in their report.

Where your child has a particularly strong opinion in favour of spending more time with one parent then it may cause a conflict between you and your ex-partner, and possibly between you and your child. Any such conflict should be handled very carefully so as not to inflame the situation or polarise either of you, or your child, further. You can see how such an opinion can be easy to either cling to in defence of your own views or be undermined, such as the other parent believing that their child has been encouraged to be of that view by the other parent. If this is an issue for you, from either side, proceed with caution and keep focused on your child's best interests. If this is an issue and you are in court proceedings, this is an example of a specific issue the CAFCASS worker will be asked to investigate and advise on in their report. It might be that you would be assisted by an appropriate expert to look further into the reasons behind the conflicting opinions and make recommendations on how to manage the situation.

VERY YOUNG CHILDREN

As a general guide, for very young children (say from newborn to toddler, but this depends on each child's own development, relationship with their other parent and needs, so this is a guide and not a rule), a common arrangement of 'little and often' is preferable. It is uncommon for very young children to spend time equally between separated parents, but that's not to say that it can't work for you if you both agree and it is what is best for your baby. For most babies, it is generally accepted that they will spend more time with one parent than the other, and that is usually the mother, for reasons such as breastfeeding or the mother commonly being the one on parental leave, and therefore physically with the baby for most of the time. For these reasons it can be harder for a young baby to be away from its mother for extended periods.

Babies need frequent contact to become familiar with and bond with people. Their daily routines of napping, feeding and stimulation are also important and require regular adjustment as the baby grows. You will need to carefully consider how the arrangements can be facilitated around your baby's routine, while balancing it against the importance of your baby's relationship with both of you. I have experienced cases involving very young children where there are disputes over breastfeeding, expressing, co-sleeping and having all the relevant kit set up for the baby in both homes. If you live close to each other post-separation this will really benefit you all in facilitating your children spending quality time with both parents. However, if a distance is involved it tends to make it much more difficult when you have a young baby.

The Historical Pattern of Care

How you as parents and as a family have cared for your children up to separation is a useful indicator of what pattern of care your children are used to and comfortable with, but after separation that pattern of care will not always translate across two homes. Managing a change in circumstances, taking into account your children's particular needs and what is possible for your new family set-up, need to be considered as part of the Welfare Checklist. How your children will be affected by the changes should be anticipated, and it is here that parents often come into dispute. You might both agree that there will need to be a change from the pattern of historical care, but it is in considering the options for that new pattern of care and how your children will cope with those changes that you might disagree.

I always discuss with my clients what their children's daily and weekly routines are like. Traditionally, the parent who spends most time with their children has been referred to as the 'primary carer'. There has been a shift away from using this term because it suggests an inequality in the parents' status, and by labelling one parent in this way sends a message that that one parent is favoured or has more say. Neither parent's opinion automatically trumps the other. But, the most reasonable, child-focused opinion will be more likely to be the right outcome. You can see how that viewpoint is more easily achieved by the parent who spends the majority of time with their children as they have more exposure to and understanding of their needs. The historical pattern of care is not decisive but it is useful to understand what your children are used to and how your family dynamic has worked for the children's care to date.

Your separation is a significant change to your children's lives and often my clients wish to prioritise keeping their children stable post-separation by keeping as close as possible to the pattern of care to which they are accustomed. By maintaining the arrangements for things such as who takes the children to school and collects them on certain days, and taking them to their usual activities and social events can assist with that stability and therefore reduce the chances of the changes to their lives impacting too significantly on them. The logistics of your two homes or interim living arrangements will have some bearing on whether this will work post-separation.

It is often the case that post-separation the historically more 'absent' parent may now make changes to their lifestyle to enable them to become more present by doing things such as making a flexible working request so that they can work from home one day a week, enabling them to partake in school drop-offs or pick-ups, or even changing their job to free up time which they now want to spend with their children. The common reaction from the other parent is to think critically that 'they never did that before', and they find it annoying that they are willing to make such changes post-separation. The fact is, your separation has probably been the trigger to such changes and, as annoying as it may initially seem to the other parent, a judge will be looking at these proposals from the perspective of whether it is in the children's best interests. It does not necessarily matter if the parent was not willing or able to do it before, what matters is your children and whether these proposed changes are good for them.

I often tell my clients to be prepared for the other parent to change their ways and perhaps put in effort that they had not during the relationship. It is obvious that such changes will invoke an emotional response and raise questions like 'Why couldn't you have done this when we were together?' and 'Are you only doing this now to get at me or influence the judge?'. If you're struggling with this change in parenting from your ex-partner, that is understandable, but your annoyance will make little difference if it is not child-focused. You will be the only one who suffers from your feelings of annoyance or upset. Try to rationalise the cause of those feelings, and sift out concerns which are genuinely related to your children's welfare rather than air your own emotional response.

Your Children's Health and Special Needs

Your children's unique needs may make a difference to how they can spend time with both of you. You will need to think of a practical solution to enable your child who has a special need to spend time with both of you, or this issue may be one of the reasons why your child spends more time with one parent than the other. An example may be where the child has a significant medical issue or disability that requires extra care and one parent works fewer hours or does not work at all to accommodate that requirement. On separation that specific care need must be catered for when deciding the arrangement for your child to spend time between the two homes. You should ask yourself if it possible for both you and your ex-partner to meet your child's extra needs.

A common health concern that I see a lot when discussing arrangements for children is a child's anxiety. The parents' separation, the change in their living arrangements or the absence of a parent living at home is frequently raised as the cause(s) of a child's anxiety, which tends to also mean they do not want to leave one parent in particular or spend time in a new home. I have seen this issue from both parents' perspectives. The parent whom the child now has anxiety about leaving does not know how to make the child spend time with the other parent or in their new home without worsening their child's anxiety issues or losing their trust. This can be further complicated if there are siblings, which raises concerns about not wanting the child to feel left out or treated differently, which may then make the anxiety worse. On the flip side, the parent who is being told that their child has anxiety often believes that it is being exaggerated by the other parent to frustrate the child's relationship with them and often report that when the child has been with them they have shown no signs of anxiety.

The only real way to work through these types of health issues is to consult with the appropriate experts. Talk to your child's GP, who may refer you on to support such as counselling or therapy, or on to a specialist consultant. Family therapy sessions can be used in situations where a child's anxiety is a concern and, if it is being recommended in your child's situation, you should engage with it, even if you do not believe that the anxiety is sufficiently bad to warrant it. It is much better to engage in any expert recommendations than refuse, because if your dispute about the arrangements for your children does end up being dealt with in court it will assist you for a judge to see that you have been willing to engage with an expert and have put your children's welfare first.

Capability of Parenting

How capable each parent is in caring for the children will be considered as part of the Welfare Checklist. Criticism of the other parent's capability is often raised in disputes about the arrangements for the children. I think this is to be expected to some extent, as when you were together there are likely to have been times when your views on parenting differed, and the fact that your relationship has broken down is indicative of you being on different pages, for whatever reason. Therefore, it's quite likely that you could each critique the other's ability to parent.

However, you must recognise the very significant difference between having a different parenting style to your ex-partner and their ability to parent being so poor that it places your children's welfare at risk. Often parents get tangled in a dispute about each other's capabilities and I think it is important for you to consider as early on as possible what the threshold is for the difference in parenting styles and a welfare concern. The question to ask yourself is this: is your ex-partner capable of meeting your children's needs? If so, it's important to respect your ex-partner's choice to parent as they see fit. You must focus on your children's welfare and whether their needs can be met while in the other parent's care before any criticism of their parenting is made. If you make criticism of your ex-partner then you might expect to get some back. This cyclical approach by both of you is only going to worsen your relationship, make communication between you tense and set a poor tone for your ongoing co-parenting. Criticising your ex-partner is unlikely to reflect well on you and it is part of the reason why it is important for you to think carefully about any criticisms you might have before you commit them to speech or writing.

Genuine welfare concerns about your ex-partner's parenting capabilities, such as them being intoxicated while your children are in their care, their physical chastisement of your children, or their inability to recognise and therefore meet your children's needs, will need to be properly safeguarded against. If you and your ex-partner are not in court proceedings, but you have concerns about your children's welfare when they are in the care of the other parent, you will need to consider what safeguards, if any, could be put in place to allow your children to spend time with the other parent safely. Safeguards can include:

- you or someone else being present (or at least in the same room) during the children's time with their other parent
- limiting their time together to, say, a few hours as opposed to a day, or to daytime hours only (not to stay overnight)
- restricting who else is present (if your concern is about a risk posed by another person being allowed to have contact with your children)
- requiring any such time to take place in a contact centre (see page 134)

It is unlikely that your ex-partner will agree that your concerns about their capabilities are accurate, and if they will not agree to your reasonable proposals for safeguarding, you will need to seriously consider whether it is proportionate and safe for you to allow your children to spend time with their other parent without the safeguards you want. If you do not agree, you can tell your ex-partner that you will not facilitate the contact they seek while your concerns are not safeguarded. That is not to say that you can stop all contact, just the aspect which you believe puts your children at risk of harm.

It will then be for your ex-partner to make an application to court for a 'child arrangements order', and you will have to explain your views and actions in those court proceedings (but remember the requirement to attend a mediation MIAM first – see page 84). It can be very difficult for you to judge what actions are reasonable in these situations and there is no black-and-white answer, so if you are in doubt you should take advice from a family lawyer. If matters do progress to court proceedings, CAFCASS will be instructed to investigate and it is likely they will be asked to report on those concerns. If the concerns are complex or significant, it might be that an expert, such as a medical expert or psychologist, is also required to assess and report (the cost of which will likely be yours to share with your ex-partner, or yours to pay entirely, unless it is something that is covered by legal aid, if you receive it).

If you are in court over your dispute about your arrangements for your children, I think it is important to put into perspective what kinds of cases a judge might see on a daily basis. While they will likely see many parents in a dispute about the right arrangements for their children, they are likely to also have cases relating to a child being removed from very difficult and often terrible situations, to include being removed from its parents. If you are in dispute with your ex-partner because you do not agree with each other's parenting styles, consider how a judge might approach such concerns in light of their contrasting cases. I'm not saying that your concerns are not valid; I'm just saying to make sure you raise the right level of concerns if you are to pursue them through the court process. Having this sort of perspective from the start might just help you to prioritise the concerns that are likely to make a significant difference, and hold back the lesser concerns which are likely to inflame the situation without much influence on the resulting arrangements for your children.

Moving Away

If one of you wants to make a significant move – whether abroad or further afield within England and Wales – you should agree the arrangements for your children prior to that move. If you are seeking to move your children with you, meaning taking your children out of the jurisdiction of England and Wales to live (known as 'external relocation') or making a big move inside England and Wales (known as 'internal relocation') to live either for a specified period or permanently, remember that you are required by shared parental responsibility to first agree a change of your children's residence with their other parent. For a move abroad, you must obtain the other parent's prior consent in writing.

As part of this agreement, the detail of your proposed arrangements for your children to continue to spend time with the 'left behind' parent should be agreed in advance and it is unlikely that the 'left behind' parent will give their consent without having first agreed these arrangements. When making a proposal to change where your children live, you should present it to your ex-partner as a well-considered and researched proposal.

You will need to do your homework and thoroughly research the area(s) you are proposing to move to and set out all the information relevant to either maintaining your children's lifestyle or enhancing it. Your reasons behind your wish to move need to be communicated and explained, with reference to the benefits those reasons will bring to your children (and not focused solely on you). Often reasons include a job opportunity which is unlikely to become available to you if you remain living where you are which might, for example, have a financial benefit or lifestyle benefit to your children, or living closer to family. Sometimes a new partner is the reason for the move and, if this is the case, you must be very cautious about how you approach this proposal. Your relationship with your new partner will need to be established, have longevity to it and be committed. A move for a relationship should be enhanced by explaining any other advantageous reasons, such as better job prospects, schooling or lifestyle benefit, and not just because *you* want to do it. The priority will be your children's welfare and not your own relationship.

The move needs to be genuinely motivated and not with the aim of distancing your children from their other parent. If your ex-partner is asking for your permission for them to relocate with your children, focus on their reasoning and your children's best interests, how well researched they are and how they propose to continue to encourage and facilitate your children's ongoing relationship with you. Think about your objections or concerns and discuss what might be put in place for you to overcome those concerns and a compromised position reached. You can request safeguards to be put in place, for example, if you have a concern about an international move and your ability to have your children returned to England and Wales if your ex-partner does not uphold the agreement. A family lawyer's advice should be taken if this is a concern to you as the safeguards will be bespoke to the intended destination country. If you believe that the move is not child-focused and is with the intent of denying you and your children a relationship then you should swiftly obtain advice from a family lawyer to assist you in dealing with the situation and to prevent the possible risk of your children being moved without your consent (see also page 175).

The parent proposing the move might expect to have to take on the larger share of the burden of facilitating your children's ongoing relationship with their 'left behind' parent (see page 170 for some advice on handovers and how they should be shared). Proposals for your children to continue to spend time with the 'left behind' parent should include both physically in person and indirectly via phone calls/video calls/emails/texts, unless there are exceptional reasons not to. These logistical issues include how many times a year your children will travel to see their other parent, how many times that parent will travel to see them, for how long and how the cost of those trips will be funded. You might need to consider who will fly with your children and where that accompanying person will stay for the duration of the trip and who will fund the cost of their accommodation. You will also need to consider the handing over of travel documents and deciding who has responsibility for maintaining the passport(s) and the cost of renewals when they become due.

Remember that choosing nurseries/schools is a decision about which, under your shared parental responsibility, you are required to consult with your ex-partner. You should investigate the area by going in advance, attending your short-listed nurseries/schools and finding out whether a place would be available for your children. If your children participate in hobbies or are encouraged by one or both parents to be part of a particular religion you should research whether it is possible for them to maintain those in the new location. If your move is to a country where a different language is spoken you should also set out your proposals for your children to learn that new language. If a child has a particular health need, you must make sure that the health requirement can be met in the new location.

Think about the timing of your proposal to relocate and raise it with your ex-partner well in advance of your intended move date. If you cannot obtain your ex-partner's written consent following direct communication you should swiftly move to mediation and/or instruct a family lawyer to set out your detailed proposal in writing to your ex-partner. If this does not enable an agreement to be reached, a court application will need to be made.

CHAPTER 10

Logistics

H OW YOUR GENERAL routine of care for your children worked when you were together might not translate easily post-separation. This applies to situations where you both remain living under the same roof and also to where you live in separate homes. The main logistical issues for you to consider when thinking about the arrangements for your children are:

- Where will you each live?
- Where will handovers take place?
- Who will do the handovers?
- Your children's belongings
- Indirect contact such as telephone calls, letters/emails/ texts, video calls, photos
- The presence of new partners/extended family members/friends

All of the above need to be considered with reference to the Welfare Checklist (see page 137), but I think logistics particularly need to be considered in light of your children's physical, emotional and educational needs, and the likely effect of any change in circumstances upon them.

Living Under the Same Roof

If you remain living under the same roof it is more likely to be possible for you to keep to a similar pattern of care that you had in place before, thereby minimising the change in circumstances and hopefully therefore any immediate effect on your children. Your children's belongings remain in one place, they have access to both of you throughout the week (depending on your agreed arrangements, of course) and, financially (which is one of the main reasons why ex-partners make this option work), the family continues to pay for just one home.

However, living under the same roof does come with its difficulties. The first will depend on what your children understand of what is going on and whether they know you are separated. If they know you are separating or separated but you seem to be continuing like a family unit as before, it might be sending them conflicting messages and confusing them. It is also prolonging the inevitable if your intention is that your separation becomes permanent. Bear in mind your children's emotional needs and seek professional assistance from a counsellor, therapist or your child's GP if you think you might need some guidance on how best to manage this situation.

While the focus should be on your children, you must also think practically about the impact of the arrangements upon you and your ex-partner. Do you feel comfortable being around your ex-partner when your children are present and 'carrying on like normal' to some extent, when the reality is that it is not normal? If you are miserable, is maintaining such an arrangement really in the best interests of your children? How you feel and how you are able to behave due to still living with your ex-partner impacts upon your children. Your emotional welfare will have a direct link to their emotional welfare and that is why your health and ability to continue living with your ex-partner is important when making this decision.

If your relationship with your ex-partner involved or continues to involve abuse either between you or with your children, it is very important to consider all available options to remove you and your children from that situation. Remaining living together, albeit separated, is unlikely to be a good idea. The Welfare Checklist expressly states that what is best for your children's welfare includes considering any harm they have suffered or are at risk of suffering. If you as the parent have suffered harm or are at risk of suffering harm from your ex-partner then, again, that forms part of the considerations for your children. Placing you at harm or at risk of harm will likely impact on your children and therefore the parent's risk is directly related to the children's welfare.

For some clients who are temporarily separated while they work on reconciling, this kind of 'carrying on as normal' can work as their children's lives remain stable, and actually working together to care for your children might help you to rebuild your relationship. If part of the breakdown of your relationship has been caused by issues about the care of your children, it will be vital to the success of your reconciliation to communicate with each other about those issues. I recommend agreeing a pattern of care, in the same way as I am advising you should if you separate permanently, between you so that you both have the same understanding and match your expectations of each other.

For those who are having to stay under the same roof for financial reasons but know that they would rather be living separately, this type of arrangement has the potential to be awkward and a cause of tension between you. I recommend trying to agree some subtle boundaries around caring for your children while you are both in the same home, such as agreeing which one of you will help with your children's home-work and/or the bedtime routine on each night of the week, and agreeing in advance the arrangements for the weekend so that you aren't both unsure, and then potentially in dispute, over who is caring for your children on the day.

Respecting those arrangements, and each other's time with the children, is vital. Very often my clients say that they are struggling to come to an arrangement with their ex-partner because they do not want to separate, or they agree that the relationship has ended but they are struggling to come to terms with it and therefore it is difficult to get them to agree on any type of arrangement. This is often because of their own feelings about your separation, not because they are gen-uinely trying to be difficult about the children. When listening to clients recount discussions or arguments, or when reading emails/text message exchanges between them, it is often very clear that the 'resisting parent' is hurt, angry, upset and feeling like they are without control, and by resisting they are at least able to grasp at some control, even if it is not actually the outcome they want. These feelings then override reasonable-ness and are why clients then come to me.

Clients often say to me, 'I don't know what else to do, what more can I say?'. In this situation, changing how you commu-nicate or switching to a different type of non-court dispute resolution method, as discussed in Chapters 4 and 5, may help you to move forward. Remember that the focus is on the best interests of your children's welfare and so, if the relationship between you has broken down to such an extent that you are unable to agree on the interim or long-term plan of living under the same roof, how successful is living under the same roof going to be for you both? The impact of the arrangements upon each of you, the atmosphere between you in the home, any tensions which might boil over and the extent to which those tensions put anyone in the family at harm or at risk of harm must all be considered as part of the overall balancing exercise.

Two Homes

If you have separated, even temporarily, and you are now living in separate homes, the distance between you and the ability to travel easily between homes, nursery/school and your respective places of work will factor into what arrangements can work for your family post-separation. If you have separated with little distance between you then a pattern of care for your children along similar lines to what was in place prior to your separation might work well. This would also hopefully be an arrangement which you feel reduces any impact of the change in circumstances on your children.

By continuing to live within a short distance of each other, the advantage should be that you will each be able to regularly engage in your children's lives and partake in their care on a more frequent basis. One of the presumptions in law is that it is in your children's best interests to have involvement from both of their parents in their life. This is explained in The Children Act as 'involvement of some kind, either direct or indirect, but not any particular division of a child's time'. It has also been set out in other people's court cases that judges believe it to be your children's right to have meaningful participation of both parents in their upbringing. I always stress this to clients – it is a child's right to a relationship with both parents, not a parent's right to a relationship with a

THE FAMILY LAWYER'S GUIDE TO SEPARATION AND DIVORCE

child. I'm stressing this here because by correctly setting your expectations and emphasising the importance of the use of the correct terminology, you should find, at the very least, that it opens communication between you and your ex-partner, and hopefully means that a child-focused plan is agreed between you.

By living close to each other there is an increased chance that you are both able to be meaningfully involved in your children's day-to-day lives, the practicalities of which will depend on your own lives and the logistics of juggling all of the demands on each of you. Each of you will need to consider how you can both balance spending time with your children with your own responsibilities, such as work, and managing things such as the school drop-offs/pick-ups, and hobbies (your children's and your own).

I have heard on multiple occasions concerns of one parent when they say that during their relationship they took quite traditional stereotypical roles, in that one would work full-time and the other would work part-time or not at all so that they were able to meet the majority of the childcare needs, and yet upon separation the parent who works full-time says that they want to equally care for the children. The practicalities of this are that the job which brings in the money to fuel the family cannot in most situations be given up or reduced. You must think carefully about practicalities and logistics. Although it is understandable why, after separation, both parents might each want their children to live with them, you must think about whether that would actually work. If one parent is available to do all or the majority of the school drop-offs and pick-ups but the other parent would need to rely on a nanny, for example, it is preferable for the children to be with a parent over a nanny.

In a situation where your children are at nursery or school during the week, and one or both of you work, you need to be practical about how you can make the arrangements for your children work between you. This is a balancing act that needs to be taken into consideration alongside the Welfare Checklist, thinking about all of the factors on the checklist (see page 137) while also working out between you the practicalities of who can do the pick-ups and drop-offs. To give you some ideas, it helps to work out the arrangements by thinking about how your children's time is spent and categorising it so that you can think about whether you are both partaking in all aspects of your children's lives. Their weekends are their fun time, although most children of school age upwards tend to have weekends which include schedules for hobbies/classes and parties. Their midweek days might be school days and so their free time midweek is limited and can, too, be taken up with hobbies/classes and/or homework. Then there are the holidays, and you might each want to spend some holiday time with your children. If your children are school age, you will need to consider how their many and sometimes long non-term-time breaks are spent, to include inset days and half terms. There are also important days and special occasions, and it is important to agree how your children will spend their birthdays, any special religious festival, your birthday, and your ex-partner's, and Mother's/Father's Day.

Usually parents like to both partake in spending time with their children during their 'free days'. The most common way of allowing for weekends to be spent with both parents is to alternate weekends between you or for the weekend to be split: Saturday with Mum and Sunday with Dad, for example, but this will only work if there is minimal travel time between you. The latter arrangement can work well if you feel your children need some time to adjust or build up to spending overnights with one parent, say where there might be some initial separation anxiety or where a child has expressed a view that they do not yet want to stay overnight with their other parent.

As children's social lives can be incredibly full and demanding, their diaries must be carefully considered post-separation. If your child receives a party invite on a day that they are planned to be with their other parent I recommend passing that invite to your ex-partner for them to make the decision about whether it is accepted. This type of issue can cause a lot of friction. In a situation where one parent might not see much of their children midweek and spends alternate weekends with them, being told by the other parent that they have to take their child to another child's birthday party for three hours of their weekend might not be acceptable to them, or something they feel particularly comfortable in engaging with if they are not familiar with the other school parents.

Understandably, each parent wants autonomy over what they choose to do with their children while they are with them. Taking your children to birthday parties can take up a large part of your limited weekend time and the priority is for your children to spend time with you. The counterargument to this is that it is likely to be in a child's interest to attend friends' parties and to socialise with their peers in a non-school environment. It won't win you a popularity vote with your children if they are left out in the school playground on Monday morning. For a parent who might not be able to partake in many school drop-offs or pick-ups, attending a child's party on a weekend is also an opportunity for them to become familiar with their children's school friends and their parents and to engage in their children's school life via this alternative route.

The same theories can apply directly to hobbies and classes which your children attend on weekends. I've had a case where a judge decided that a child should only attend football practice and matches on alternate weekends because it was too onerous on the weekend to expect the parent who did not see the child during the week to have half of the weekend overrun by the child participating in sport. You can see there is no right answer here – it will all depend on the application of the Welfare Checklist, your relationship with your ex-partner and how willing you are to both collaborate to ensure your arrangement works for your children.

If you both live close to your children's school(s), it might be possible for you both to spend time with them during the week. There are polarised and quite traditional views which are often brought up when I discuss these arrangements with clients. A more traditional view is that the children should stay in the same home on weekdays so that they are kept stable, all their belongings required for school and after-school activities are kept in the same location, the children are not moved midweek between two homes, and their routine can be kept consistent every night. This argument is put forward with the view that it benefits the children so that they are not tired, missing any necessary school or hobby equipment and they feel calm and safe. The counter to this is that children can have two homes – both parents are still parents and are able to parent their children and do their homework and bedtime routines just as well as the other parent. School uniforms can be bought for both homes, sports kits can move with the children between both homes and routines can be replicated in both homes. The parents who have trust in each other, and working lives which allow for both parents to be involved midweek, tend to be able to make midweek overnight stays between two homes work. Another option is to alternate weeks between parents' homes with handovers on a weekend.

It is important for your children, but also for both parents, to agree on a plan and stick to it. The routine of that arrangement needs time to embed, for all of you, and the repetition of the arrangement over months will help your children to settle into their new norm. If you and your ex-partner stick to the precise arrangements, without introducing flexibility too soon, it shows respect and reliability, and keeps the new routine stable for your children. If you have been critical of your ex-partner, or if you are the one to have been criticised for not being reliable, if you have consistently been on time and turned up when agreed, say for six months, it will be difficult for that criticism to continue to be raised. Trust is vital to good co-parenting and if it means proving yourself, whether you think it is justified or not, you should do it for the sake of your children and your ongoing relationship as co-parents.

Once the arrangements have been kept to for a while, you can then look to introduce some flexibility, but only if you both agree and if that flexibility is necessary or of benefit to your children. Being flexible is based on trust and is also about working together, which is why your relationship needs time for a new foundation to be laid. Judge how good your relationship is with your ex-partner before you suggest any changes or flexibility, such as switching days or times, and recognise the importance of stability and commitment to the agreed arrangements. If after a few months of trying an arrangement, one parent has not been committed or reliable it will worsen your relations, increase the tension and widen the gap between you, thus increasing the chances of you ending up in court over the dispute. It will not look good on you in court if the other parent can show that you were unreliable.

It's a good idea to keep a diary of what is going on so make contemporaneous notes of anything of importance that was said or done which impacts upon your views about the right arrangements for your children. For example, if you have agreed a trial arrangement but your ex-partner sometimes doesn't turn up or consistently returns your children to you later than the agreed time, keep a diary to record it and document that you have, politely, raised your concerns with your ex-partner. If you are the parent who keeps returning your children late, but with a valid reason, then you too should document this and write down that you have explained the reason to your ex-partner and have attempted to alleviate the cause. For example, if you agreed that you would return your children at 6pm on a Sunday but it turns out that the traffic is far worse than you had anticipated but you can't set off earlier because it means your children would not have time to eat their tea, you need to communicate these logistical issues. I recommend that you do so in writing via email or text, so that you can document that you have reasonably explained the issue and proposed a way around it. Your records may be necessary should your dispute later progress to court. They will be a useful aide-memoire for you to discuss accurately your concerns with a family lawyer, and they can be used as a basis for a statement should your dispute end up in court.

Distance between your two homes

If there is now some distance or a problematic travel route between you and your ex-partner then a change in the historical pattern of care is likely to be required. You will need to think practically about this and communicate with each other about how the logistics might work, bearing in mind the effect of those new logistical arrangements on your children.

A move out of the locality by either of you will obviously have great significance and impact upon the arrangements you can put in place for your children. You need to remember that you share parental responsibility, and therefore you must consult each other before making any significant changes to where your children will live. Even if the parent wishing to relocate is not proposing that your children should move with them, I recommend that you jointly consider how your children will maintain their relationship with that parent. Whichever parent is proposing to move, such a big decision should be done in consultation with their ex-partner.

Where there is some distance between both parents' homes it is unlikely to be possible for your children to spend time with you both midweek, especially if they are school age. As such, it is likely that your arrangement will focus on how your children will spend their weekends and holiday time with each of you. You can also build in indirect contact with your children when they are not physically with you. It can be important for your children to know that they can still access you even when they are with the other parent, and this can give them comfort and reassurance. In the intervening periods between seeing your children, you could build in telephone or video calls and letters/text messages, if age-appropriate. However, there is a balance to be struck between maintaining a good relationship with your children and being overbearing and intrusive of your children's time with their other parent. Daily telephone calls are frequently complained about as too much and a burden on the parent who needs to facilitate them. If your children are old enough to have their own mobile phone this can be both an assistance and a hindrance. It means that the arrangements for indirect contact, such as text messages and phone or video calls, can be more flexibly arranged, and your children can facilitate them with some or little supervision as appropriate. However, it can also be hard to regulate and an agreed pattern for calls does seem to benefit all.

Post-separation, the logistics of a video call might mean more than just making sure you have an Internet connection. It is common for video calls to cause a dispute between parents. Often, depending on their age and their relationship with the other parent, and even the relationship between the parents, a child can be distracted and difficult to keep focused on the video call. If the child is not of an age where they can make calls independently, the parent with the child – the 'facilitating parent' – will need to be present to encourage the child to engage or keep focused on their conversation with the other parent. The facilitating parent is therefore placing themselves firmly in the firing line should the call not be particularly long or fruitful, and the obvious person to blame for that, often unjustly, is them.

Video calling is also often disliked because of the intrusion factor. Clients have told me that they do not like video calls being arranged when their children are in their house as the other parent can then snoop into their life by seeing the inside of their home, even if it used to be their shared family home. This feeling from a video call is akin to the other parent being present in the house – an unwelcome visitor. If a video call is likely to be an issue for you, you should discuss this and see if you can build into the agreement something to overcome your concerns, such as agreeing that the video call will take place at a time when you know your children will not be in a rush to go out to an activity, but also after they have been fed so they are not grumpy and distracted. Make sure your Internet connection is strong enough for the call to take place in, for example, the child's bedroom and no other place in your home.

For international arrangements, logistics will need to cover time zone differences, availability of the Internet, and possibly the use of foreign sim cards to enable calls. Time differences should be specified and considered for when clocks change in different time zones. Covering the costs of these requirements to enable the children's indirect contact with a parent may also need to be discussed and agreed.

Handovers

As part of your consideration of and discussions about logistics you will need to agree the finer details of your arrangements, such as handovers, how to share the travel and costs of that travel if it is not shared equally or affordable. The 'handover' is where and when your children change between your and their other parent's care. There are lots of options and it will depend on the distance between you, the type of travel required and your relationship with your ex-partner.

If you do not get on well and think handovers will be difficult, with potential for argument, I recommend arranging for them to take place in a public location. Your children will be privy to any crossed words and tension, so by choosing a location in a public place, where there are plenty of other people around, it reduces the likelihood of you getting into an argument and keeps the handover child-focused. I've had clients use a range of different public locations, including supermarkets, car parks, service stations and places of work.

It might be that you would rather limit direct handovers between you, and this can be done by being creative about your arrangements. If your children attend nursery or school, for example, you can do a handover without having to see each other by one parent taking them to nursery/school in the morning and the other parent collecting them on that day. If you have an alternating weekend as part of your arrangement, this could work for both handovers if they are from school pick-up on Friday to drop-off at school on Monday. An alternative is to engage a third party to do the handovers for you. You could ask a family member or friend to transport the children between you, or at least be present during the handovers. This is a big ask for someone to undertake regularly and so it is probably only workable as an interim arrangement.

You should agree between you from the outset who will do each journey and exactly where your meeting point will be. If one parent is going to take the burden of most or all of the handovers you should discuss if they will require financial compensation. In situations where travel by train is required I recommend that you build into your discussions agreements about the purchase of train tickets in advance at cheaper rates, and agree that if any changes to the arrangements are required they must be agreed before the train tickets are purchased or the purchasing party is to be compensated if changes are made after purchase. In situations where your relationship is strained or your existing arrangement is not working for you, it is this level of detail that should be discussed and agreed to reduce any confusion and potential for disputes further down the line.

There is no set rule about how parents should share the travel and cost, but it is a common point of contention between couples. The parent who has moved away is often told that as it was their choice to move, they should have the burden of the travel and cost. However, the usual response to that is that they simply cannot afford it or they cannot always drop off and/or collect the children due to practical issues, such as work commitments. I suggest your starting point for discussion is that the travel and cost should be shared equally but usually affordability and day-to-day logistics may not make equal sharing an option for you.

It is common for handovers to take place at each other's homes. However, where one of you has remained in the former family home this can cause difficulties. One issue I hear from my clients is that the parent who has moved out returns to collect their children and lets themselves in, entering the house as if they were still living there. If this is an issue for you, even if the house is still co-owned or rented together with your ex-partner, you will need to ask them to respect your privacy and private life and to not enter the home without a formal invite, just as you would not let yourself in and make yourself at home in their new home. The other common complaint I hear is from the parent who moved out. They say that they find it very difficult to return to the former family home, given the relationship breakdown and the emotion that comes with that, and therefore it makes handovers at that location too emotive and stressful. In this situation, it will be a matter of discussing what could be done to overcome those feelings or agreeing another location for the handover. A resolution might be for that parent to wait in the car instead of coming to the door. They could call or send a text message when they arrive (at a pre-arranged time, of course) and, upon receipt of that call or message, the other parent brings the children out to the car.

Using a contact book

A common issue is that one or both parents find handovers daunting for fear of an argument or communication not being reciprocated, such as you giving details about your children but your ex-partner not offering the same information in return. I recommend using a 'contact book' to try to alleviate these issues. This is frequently used within court proceedings for parents who have such a bad level of dispute that they struggle to be able to communicate civilly with each other in a child-focused way. A contact book is just a notebook that passes between you at handover and prompts you to communicate non-verbally with each other, focusing solely on your children. You should use the book to give each other information about your children, such as how their health is, any issues that need to be communicated and/or any activity feedback or reminders. I have had clients use it to keep a food diary for a child who was weaning, noting down what and how much the child had eaten and when. If your child is sick, you should write down the doctor's advice in the book, including any guidance on when to give medicine and how much they have already had when with you.

A contact book is a clear signal that your communication has deteriorated to a poor state and it can be difficult to recover from there. The contact book itself can then become an avenue for further bad feelings towards each other. I've had many clients report that they did not wish to succumb to completing the book because they found it humiliating, especially where they do not consider themselves to be the cause of them needing the book in the first place. Others have reported that their ex-partners refuse to complete the book or hand it over at all. Remember that this disregard of the importance of communication and the inability to put your children ahead of your own feelings will not reflect well on you. If you end up in court or are already in court proceedings when using the contact book, a judge will be informed of the extent to which you have engaged in its use.

For some, the use of a contact book is a building block. The detail can start at the bare minimum, but you can work on your communication by providing more detail. The more detail you give, the better chance you have of being able to re-engage with each other and open yourselves to verbal communication again. Extra details could include such things as 'We went to the zoo today and we saw some elephants, monkeys and birds. George particularly enjoyed watching the penguins', 'We went to the park and Mason rode his bike and fed the ducks' or 'Amara has done well with her maths home-work but has struggled with her four times table'. If you actively want to use the contact book to help you to open up a verbal dialogue with your ex-partner, even if it is just a quick exchange for the benefit of your children at handover, these extra details might enable you to keep the conversation child-focused. It is not a point-scoring record, so the tone will need to be kept friendly. It is very hard to undo the damage that has caused your current inability to speak civilly to each other, so the contact book in isolation is not going to suddenly make you amicable. However, it provides an opportunity, and if you put in the effort or see the effort being made, there's a chance that something positive could come from it.

It is often the case that when parents are unable to com-municate well with each other, the children pick up on the tensions and may also feel sensitive about their communica-tions with each parent, perhaps not wanting to upset one parent by discussing things they do with the other. By adding the extra level of detail you are providing conversation-starters, if not between you and your ex-partner, but between your ex-partner and your children. If activities are recorded in the contact book, your children might feel able to communicate about things they do with one parent in the presence of the other.

I am aware that some parents think the contact book is a means to record that they think they are the better parent and write down what they think makes them look good. You know your ex-partner, so it's about judging your situation and thinking about what might help, trying to put your children's best interests first, not trying to antagonise the situation, and keeping the content and tone appropriate.

Holidays Abroad

For parents wishing to build in foreign holidays as part of their arrangements you can consider these logistics as part of your overall agreement. Remember that you must obtain the other parent's consent or the permission of the court to take your children out of England and Wales, and you should do this before you book your travel abroad. If there is a child arrangements order already in place which states that your children live with you (a 'lives with' order) or with you both (a joint 'lives with' order), then the person stated as the parent with whom the children are living, or both if it is shared, is permitted to take the children out of England and Wales for up to one month without the other parent's consent or the permission of the court. You should, of course, inform the other parent of any such plans and any consequential impact on their relationship with your children, such as organising a different weekend for your children to see that parent if they will be away when they would normally spend time with them.

It is a criminal offence and classed as child abduction to remove a child from England and Wales without the consent of the other parent with parental responsibility (or anyone else who has parental responsibility, for example, a step-parent who has parental responsibility will also need to give permission), which is punishable by imprisonment, a fine or both. It is to be taken very seriously and, for this reason, I always recommend (unless you have a court order stating that your children live with you) obtaining permission from your ex-partner in writing. A text or an email is fine, so that if your trip was ever doubted you have evidence that consent was given by your ex-partner. The Home Office has also issued guidance about travelling with children, and if your children have a different surname to you on their passport(s) you could be asked for evidence of your relationship to your children. You should therefore take your children's birth certificates with you along with a copy of the court order or evidence of permission from your ex-partner.

Simply booking a holiday and telling the other parent does not mean you will get their permission because you present it to them as a fait accompli. Likewise, you should not unreasonably withhold your consent to your ex-partner taking your children abroad on holiday. In every situation, you should inform your ex-partner of the proposed dates, where you will be staying, the travel details, such as flight numbers and times, emergency contact information and who will be with your children on that holiday. For the parent being asked to give their consent, you should remember to focus on your children's welfare and whether that holiday will be in their best interests. This is how a judge will consider it.

Rather than saying no outright, communicate the reasons why you have concerns and open up a dialogue about how those concerns might be overcome. Building in video calls and photo messages during the trip away and discussing the time-scale – for example, whether a one-week holiday would be a better starting point then a fortnight's break abroad – can all help to alleviate concerns. You might also discuss whether the location poses a risk to your children's safety or health, in which case you could agree to another location. Making compromises may be necessary to allow your trip to go ahead, and also to keep your co-parenting relationship civil with you working together rather than against each other. The process will have a more positive than negative tone and progress is more likely to be achieved.

If you and your ex-partner agree on one or both of you being able to take your children abroad on holiday, you can make an agreement to cover either the exact dates or a general pattern of holidays without knowing the exact dates, such as 'the first week of Easter to include Good Friday' or 'one week at Easter' if you can't be so precise. It will be difficult to pin down the arrangements for years to come, but you can agree a general pattern for the next 12 months, which is easier if your children are school age as it will give some structure by their non-term time availability, even if precise dates are not yet known. If you are generally agreeing arrangements such as 'ten consecutive nights during the summer break', then you should also specify a date by which those dates must be agreed each year, giving yourself plenty of time to agree the dates in advance.

When consent is not given

If, after discussions about how to make the holidays agreeable for both of you, consent is still not given, you should see if setting out your proposal in detail in solicitors' correspondence and/or attending mediation together helps. In my experience, having assistance from a family lawyer or mediator is sufficient for a resolution to be reached in most cases. However, if you cannot reach agreement and you think your ex-partner is withholding their consent unreasonably, a judge will need to be asked to give consent for you to take your children abroad on holiday in place of your ex-partner. An application to the court for a 'specific issue order' will need to be made by the parent wishing to take the children abroad, with the 'specific issue' being whether or not your children should be allowed to go on that holiday. For the parent objecting to their children being taken abroad on holiday, you could make an application to court for a 'prohibitive steps order' to ask a judge to make an order preventing the other parent from taking your children away.

You will have to think carefully about the timing of your request for your ex-partner's permission to take your children on holiday, because if their consent is unreasonably withheld you will need enough time in advance of your proposed holiday to attempt mediation first and, if that does not work, to make an application to court. You should also factor in the cost of making an application to the court. If consent is being unreasonably withheld by your ex-partner, it is rare in court proceedings relating to children's issues for a judge to make an order that the 'unreasonable parent' pays the legal costs of the parent who got the order they were seeking. Usually in children's court proceedings you will each pay for your own legal costs.

These types of orders can be used for other issues too. For example, if you cannot agree on which school your children should attend, you can apply for a specific issue order for a judge to make the decision about the best school for your children. A prohibitive steps order might be required if you want to stop your ex-partner from making a parental responsibility decision about your children, which you do not agree is in their best interests. An example of this is if you and your ex-partner have different religious beliefs and disagree about whether your children should partake in a particular religious event, for example, to prevent your children from being christened or circumcised.

Managing and Introducing New Partners

While a new partner for either or both of you should not influence your ongoing arrangements for your children, it often comes up as an issue between ex-partners as a point of conflict due to the presence of a new partner not being welcomed by the ex-partner or children. The presence of a new partner can influence whether your ex-partner is willing to encourage your children to spend time with you when they know someone else is present. Alternatively, your children may be influenced in their views about spending time with a parent depending on their relationship with that new partner.

Though I am aware of situations where ex-partners and new partners all get along and work together in co-parenting, this is not the norm and, unfortunately, new partners are often a cause of dispute. The obvious example of this being an issue is where the new partner was the person with whom they had an affair, from which the parents' relationship broke down. It's worth noting, though, that most issues come, not from the existence of a new relationship, but from how that new partner was introduced to the children.

The introduction of a new partner should be discussed between parents first. It's unlikely to be an easy or even welcomed conversation, but it is much better to engage with each other over when and how the new partner should be introduced, than for it to happen unexpectedly and cause upset. My advice is that new partners should not be introduced to your children until that new relationship is stable and has a feel of permanency and longevity to it, as a rough indication, perhaps at least six months, but it will depend on each relationship's own progression. To introduce a new partner early on in a relationship has the potential to be confusing and destabilising to your children if that new relationship then breaks down. Your children will build a relationship with that new partner but it is contingent on your relationship with that person being successful.

If the new relationship has only been in existence for a short time, rather volatile in nature or is not expected to continue into your reasonably foreseeable future, I do not recommend introducing that new partner to your children yet. In many of my cases my client's ex-partner has clearly thought about these considerations and decided not to introduce their new partner to their children as their 'new partner'. Instead of introducing them as their new partner they have thought that they could get around it by introducing them as 'their friend' instead. Of course, a parent should be able to judge whether their children should be introduced to their friends, but if that 'friend' seems to be consistently or increasingly present during the time that their children spend with them it is likely to become obvious that that person is more than just a friend. This will become an issue because the ex-partner feels like something underhand has taken place – a big decision about introducing their children to a new partner has been made without their input and has been done in an insincere manner which has immediate trust consequences.

How a new partner is introduced to your children should be discussed with your ex-partner and will depend on your children's age, understanding and what you feel is appropriate for them. Your ex-partner need not be present when your new partner is introduced to them, unless this is something you want. It's common for a new partner to be introduced and spend increasing amounts of time with the children before any significant steps are taken, such as them moving in. There is no set answer for how you should introduce a new partner, and if you are worried about how you should do it or how your ex-partner might do it, then perhaps you could jointly seek the assistance of a counsellor or mediator to work through it together.

In a situation where trust has been damaged as a consequence of a new partner being introduced to your children without your prior knowledge or consent, in addition to communicating your concerns to your ex-partner you should consider what you want them to do to rebuild your trust in them. Would attending counselling or therapy with you assist as a platform for that breach of trust to be addressed, with the hope that by your ex-partner understanding the impact of their actions it might avoid repeated damaged in the future? Other options might include attending, either together or separately, a parenting course for separated parents. There are many courses on offer from different angles, but a commonly attended course (and often one parents are ordered to attend as part of court proceedings) is the Separated Parents Information Programme, offered by CAFCASS and aimed at helping separated parents understand how to avoid conflict, improve communication and cope with the emotion and conflict of co-parenting.

Finally, though you may not initially like the thought of it, perhaps being introduced to and spending some time with the new partner might make you feel better about their ongoing involvement with your children.

Formalising Agreed Child Arrangements

The majority of parents are able to agree the arrangements for their children between them without court proceedings being necessary. If you have reached agreement with your ex-partner, you are not required in law to formalise those agreed terms; it is sufficient for both of you to have just agreed. You can immediately start your new arrangements and need not do anything other than build on it by being reliable, reasonable and civil.

The court's approach to children's arrangements has been to avoid making court orders, preferring to trust the children's parents to be able to sensibly manage and agree the best interests of their children. If your agreement relates to a significant parental responsibility issue, such as allowing one or both of you to travel abroad with your children and it has been particularly difficult for you to get there and reach agreement on that issue, I would lean towards having your agreement approved by the court and turned into a consent order (by joint agreement). If you have reached this agreement having gone around in circles many times before with your ex-partner, and you don't quite trust their long-term commitment, the extra weight of it being made into a consent order is likely to assist you both.

Despite not needing to formalise your agreement, I recommend that you at least have it written down in an email between you to make sure that you are both of the same interpretation and understanding. If you are amicable and trust that you will both keep to your side of the agreed arrangements, that is all you need to do. If you have reached a verbal agreement, putting it in writing between you either in an email or in a more formal 'parenting plan' style document will reduce the chances of either of you having misunderstood or reinterpreting what had been agreed.

A parenting plan is a template document which helps you to reflect and record your agreed arrangements for your children. You can obtain a copy of the template from the CAFCASS website (www.cafcass.gov.uk/grown-ups/parenting-plan.aspx). It is not necessary to complete a parenting plan if you are both happy to simply record your agreement in an email, but if you want it to feel more formal, and perhaps want some assistance in making sure you have considered all the important issues, the template can really give you that methodical approach. If you reached agreement in mediation, your mediator will produce a similar style parenting agreement with you at the conclusion of your mediation process.

Whether you use direct negotiation, solicitor negotiation, mediation, collaborative law or arbitration to resolve your dispute, once you have agreed the terms of your settlement you can convert those agreed terms in an order for approval by the court, making it an enforceable court order. You will need a solicitor to draft what is called a 'consent order', so that the terms are properly set out and drafted to have the correct legal effect. Once you and your ex-partner agree to the drafting of the consent order you can send the consent order to the court for a judge to approve it and make it a formal order of the court. You can do all this without actually needing to set foot in a court. One of you will need to take the lead and be the 'applicant', and complete 'Form C100: Apply for a court order to make arrangements for a child or resolve a dispute about their upbringing', which you can obtain from the court or form the government's website. You will need to tick the box to say that it is an application to make an order by consent and attach to the form a draft of the order you are asking a judge to approve. There is a court fee for the application (which is, at the time of writing, £215), and you will need to pay the fee when you send in your application. CAFCASS will be required to perform their standard background checks (as explained on page 140), but once received, and assuming they do not highlight any welfare concerns, a judge can be asked to approve the order for you.

The effect of a consent order means there is a potential for penalties if the terms of the order are significantly breached by either parent, although it is only in situations of significant or serious breaches that any penalties would be handed out by a judge. The real benefit of having a consent order for child arrangements is that it gives you both the clear message and understanding that your agreement is formal and gives you set boundaries which you are less likely to push because of its formality. You are both more likely to respect the terms of a court order than a quick text messaged agreement informally made between you. If your agreed arrangements include permission for one or both of you to travel abroad with your children it is advantageous to have it reflected in a consent order and you should take a copy of it with you when you travel abroad as evidence that you are not committing child abduction (assuming you are travelling within the terms of your consent order).

Changing Child Arrangements

Whether you have an agreement in place or a formal court order which sets out the arrangements for your children, you and your ex-partner can change these arrangements by agreement at any time, either on a temporary basis (such as swapping weekends) or long-term. You do not need to return to court to change a court order if the changes are by agreement, but I recommend setting the changes out in an email between you so that you each have a record of them and confirm you share the same understanding.

If you do not agree to the change of arrangements you will need to start the process of formalising the dispute and follow my guidance about starting with non-court dispute resolution methods (see Chapter 5). If one of you is seeking to vary the terms of a child arrangements order (either one imposed upon you by the court, or a consent order) then, unless there is an emergency and it is reasonable for you to make an urgent variation, you must keep to the terms of the order until a judge has approved a variation. You will need to make a formal application to the court for a variation of a child arrangements order.

The usual prompts for a change of child arrangements are because the initial agreement was made without knowing whether it would work and so a natural review process will take place as a type of 'trial and error' followed by a tweaking of the arrangements rather than a complete overhaul. A significant change in your children's lives might also be a prompt for review, such as starting school and therefore adding in a new logistical dimension to the arrangements. As your children get older the amount of time spent with both parents might also change and this is one of the main reasons for a parent to seek a variation, and for disputes to occur. Be mindful of your children's own views which will start to carry more weight as they mature. When considering a variation of arrangements for a child, do it with reference to the Welfare

Checklist and the considerations I have previously advised (see Chapter 9).

Remember, if you do not agree to a variation then you should keep to the existing arrangements. If in doubt, send a message or an email in advance of the next handover to confirm your understanding of what will happen, and if there is genuine concern about a risk of harm to your children, seek immediate professional assistance. Avoid saying to each other 'my lawyer says' or 'I'll see you in court' unless you have genuinely spoken to your lawyer and what you are passing on is truthful, or unless you really have made an application to court (and complied with the mediation MIAM requirements first). Using such intimidation tactics doesn't work – it heightens the temperature unnecessarily and reduces the chances of you being able to reach a compromised resolution.

CHAPTER 11

Financial Support for Children

A PARENT WHOSE CHILD lives in England and Wales, and who does not have their child living with them for at least 50 per cent of their child's time (which is taken as an average over a year), has a legal responsibility to pay maintenance for their child. A 'child' in this context is under the age of 16, or under the age of 20 and in full-time education (up to and including the equivalent of A levels, but not higher), or living with a parent who receives child benefit for them. The maintenance, or 'child periodical payments' as they can also be known, is payable to the parent with whom the child lives for most of their time.

It is for that parent to use their discretion in spending the maintenance to meet their child's financial needs to include (but this list is just indicative and not conclusive) the child's:

- food
- housing expenses
- personal care
- medication
- educational expenses
- hobbies and activities

Child maintenance is payable whether the child's parents were married or unmarried, and it has no connection to whether the parent has parental responsibility for the child. This means that an absent parent (someone who has spent no or very little time with the child), who might not even be named on the child's birth certificate and was not married to the child's other parent, is still liable to pay child maintenance. It is payable regardless of their past and ongoing relationship with the other parent or their child.

The Child Maintenance Service (CMS), as it is currently known, though you may have heard it referred to as The Child Support Agency, sets out and applies the formula for calculating how much maintenance should be paid, and can also be involved in connected arrangements, such as locating a parent who needs to pay, getting the money from the paying parent and transferring the money between parents. The CMS website (https://childmaintenanceservice.direct.gov.uk) is brilliant and explains all about child maintenance. It also has an online calculator which is easy to use and, after answering just a few simple questions, it will tell you how much maintenance needs to be paid on a weekly basis.

If you and your ex-partner are able to talk between you about financial support for your children, then I recommend that you use the CMS's online calculator to work it out for you. There is no point in you agreeing an amount lower than the CMS's calculation as there is a set formula that is set out in law, and therefore the paying parent has a legal obligation to pay that amount as a minimum. You do not actually need to engage the CMS about your maintenance, you can simply use the calculator to tell you the amount payable and then between you set up a direct debit so that amount is then regularly paid as due. For a lot of parents this is how easy it can be to sort out child maintenance. It is one of the only areas of family law where discretion is not applied and the set formula is the answer (for most cases). I'll explain more about when discretion can be applied in the next paragraph.

Most receiving parents are of the view that the set formula is not particularly generous and it is often the case that it is not enough to meet the children's actual expenses. For parents who are civil with each other, it might be that you can talk about a flexible arrangement, such as where an agreed monthly amount of maintenance is paid, and for more costly expenses for your children you agree that additional contributions will be made. If the paying parent receives more than £156,000 gross (before paying tax) per year in income, they are over the limit of the amount of income to which the formula will apply, and if agreement cannot be reached between parents about additional funds being made available to meet the children's financial needs, you can consider making an application to the court for a 'top-up' of maintenance. A 'top-up' application is where a court can use discretion to make an order that the paying parent must pay extra money in addition to the CMS set amount to meet the children's needs (see also page 190).

The 'top-up' element is discretionary as it will be calculated with reference to your children's specific needs, which you will need to itemise, and it is not in line with a strict formula. If you are a paying parent who earns above the current £156,000 gross per year income threshold and you are being asked by your ex-partner to contribute more than the CMS calculated amount for your children, I recommend that you ask for a schedule and evidence of your children's financial needs, and what the other parent's deficit is after deducting your CMS contributions and their own affordable contribution from their income. The deficit is a rough guide to quantifying what your children's additional 'needs' are and you should try to either compromise and reach agreement together or use non-court dispute resolution methods to reach agreement (see Chapter 5), otherwise you will need a judge to decide the outcome in court, but remember this only applies to those who might qualify for 'top up' maintenance.

To use the CMS formula, you will need to agree what the paying parent's gross weekly income is, which means how much money they receive on average a week before they pay tax and National Insurance, although money deducted from their pay as pension contributions is allowed to be deducted from the calculation. The amount is adjusted depending on:

- How many children you have together and therefore how many the paying parent needs to pay maintenance to you for.
- How many other children the paying parent pays maintenance for.
- The number of nights a week the children stay with the paying parent on average over a year. The more nights on average over a week, the bigger the discount as the paying parent will have to pay for the children when they are in their care. This needs to be taken as an average over the year so that holiday periods are included as part of the calculation and not just the usual weekly arrangements.

If you are the parent who is due to receive the child maintenance and you do not get on well with your ex-partner or if it is difficult to locate them, you might not know information about their income to enable you to use the online CMS calculator. If you are in contact with your ex-partner you should ask them for a copy of their most recent P60 and/or tax return so that you can see for yourself what it is they earn. If they will not voluntarily disclose their income to you, you will need to engage the CMS to do this for you. Often this assists parents who are not able to communicate very well as it removes the need for you to communicate directly with each other. The CMS will be the go-between and do the work for you.

The CMS charges a small fee for doing this, and if you also want them to collect the money from your ex-partner and pay it to you, they also charge fees for this extra service. This 'collect and pay' service is optional and, usually, it is sufficient to have the CMS calculate the amount to be paid and then the payment of it can be arranged between you. I advise setting up a direct debit or standing order. As the child maintenance calculation produces a weekly amount you can either pay weekly or, if you prefer to pay monthly, you will need to convert that weekly amount into a monthly amount to pay by a monthly direct debit. You can do this by multiplying the weekly amount by 52 (the number of weeks in a year) and dividing it by 12 (the number of months in a year).

It is a common allegation that the paying parent manipulates their income so that the calculation produces a lower liability then what the receiving parent believes they should rightly pay. There is an option to challenge the CMS calculation and the dissatisfied parent should consider whether to make a 'variation' application. An example of this is where a paying parent's calculation has been done only on their earned income and they have further income from unearned sources, such as property rental income or investment income. If your ex-partner receives income through alternative sources, such as a company, investments or property rental from either England and Wales or abroad, this should be disclosed in their tax return, which is why you should request a copy if you think your ex-partner's income may come from sources beyond employment, or if they are a high earner. Unearned income is not automatically included as part of the CMS assessment, but by making a variation application any such unearned income can then be included as part of the paying parent's gross income. An increase in the gross income will increase the liability for child maintenance. If you engage the CMS to do the assessment for you they can obtain the information about your ex-partner's income from HMRC. For any nuisances or issues to do with maintenance I advise that you discuss them with the CMS and take the advice of a family lawyer to assist you.

It is worth noting that if, as part of a financial settlement on divorce, you agreed and it is reflected in a court order the amount your ex-spouse must pay for child maintenance, neither of you are able to apply to the CMS to reassess the agreed payable amount until 12 months after the date of the consent order. If more than a year has passed since the date of your financial settlement court order, and you think there has been a change to either your own or your ex-spouse's circumstances which might warrant a change to the amount you either receive or pay in child maintenance, you can choose to apply to the CMS to assess how much should be paid, taking into account the most up-to-date information. This would be done in the hope that it will either increase the amount you receive or, if you are the paying parent struggling to meet the payments, reduce the amount payable.

Immediate Financial Considerations

Whether you are married or unmarried, and if married, whether you decide to divorce now or in the future, you will need to figure out quite quickly, upon separation, how to manage your finances. It can be a big flare point for arguments and unless you are a family lawyer it is very difficult to know where you stand and what is fair, and trust in each other can become an issue.

The initial advice I give to clients, regardless of their marital status, is to maintain the status quo as much as they can. This will be possible if you continue to live under the same roof, but may not be so easy if your money must stretch further to cover the costs of a second home. The priority will be in making sure your children's needs are met first and the money will therefore have to be spent on maintaining the security of their home and outgoings. Think carefully before making any knee-jerk changes to your family's finances, such as stopping direct debits or removing children from private school, and do not make any unilateral financial decisions, even if it is about money held or earned solely by you (this is particularly the case if you are married).

Maintaining the status quo means making sure all of your existing direct debits and usual spending continues to be met by each of you as they were while you were together. If you have a home, mortgage or other loans together remember that you are jointly responsible for the mortgage and bills in your joint names, and moving out of the home will not automatically release you from those responsibilities. You will need to notify your utility providers and provide meter readings, and inform your Local Authority of your new status for changes to your council tax (see page 236). Nevertheless, there is likely to be an ongoing need for you to financially support each other in this interim period, especially so if you have children together or are married.

Unless and until you have worked out how you will each move on following your separation, you should agree to maintain the status quo. If there is any difficulty over this, you should swiftly seek advice from a family lawyer who will be able to explain how the law applies to you (remember it applies differently to married and unmarried couples) and what your options are to preserve your interim financial position.

Married Parents

If you are married to your ex-partner you can deal with your children's financial needs beyond maintenance as part of your financial settlement on divorce (see Chapter 13).

Unmarried Parents

If you are not married to your ex-partner you should consider with a family lawyer whether you can make a claim against your ex-partner under Schedule 1 Children Act 1989 ('Schedule 1'). As you are unmarried you have limited claims, if any, against your ex-partner for you own financial needs, but the law does make provision for children of an unmarried couple to have their financial needs met, such as housing provision, extra maintenance, school fees and any needs arising out of disability. Remember that this is discretionary and dependent on your ex-partner's finances, so advice from a family lawyer is recommended to get an idea of what might apply in your circumstances.

Under Schedule 1, a parent on behalf of their child, a person acting formally in a capacity as a parent for a child (such as a guardian) or the child themselves (which is rare in practice) can apply for one or more of the following financial provisions to meet the child's financial needs:

'Top-up' child maintenance

You can apply for 'top-up' maintenance if the paying parent has income of over £156,000 gross per year and a child has financial needs that are not met by the CMS assessed amount for child maintenance alone. The amount claimed by the receiving parent will need to be reasonable in the circumstances of that particular child, which will take into consideration the standard of living that child was used to when its parents were together or in reference to the respective parents' own standards of living. For example, this type of application is often brought by an unmarried mother of limited or average wealth against the much wealthier father of her child. It is likely to be considered as part of such a situation that the child should not suffer a huge disparity in standard of living between its parents.

The application is made for the child's financial needs only. There is no provision for an unmarried parent to make claims against their ex-partner for their own financial needs, although there is limited scope for some funds to be provided to that parent in compensation for their care of the child, such as in a situation where they have been unable to undertake employment to care for the child.

Housing provision

It is possible for a court to order the wealthier parent to transfer money to the other parent for them to purchase a property to live with the child or, alternatively, they could be ordered to transfer an already owned property to the other parent. The property will not belong to the claiming parent forever – the property or money will revert to the original owning parent at a set date in the future, which is often when the child turns 18 years old or finishes full-time education.

School/training fees

An order can be made for a parent to pay for all or some of their child's school or vocational training fees and say whether it is for a specific number of terms/years, or until the child finishes their education. This may be private school fees or, for example, a photography course for the purposes of furthering the child's training. You will need to be confident that the paying parent can afford to meet such outgoings before you make such a claim, and do not commit to a private school or a training course without an agreement or court order confirming the other parent's contribution or commitment to pay their contribution or the fees in full.

Lump sums

Debts incurred or money anticipated to be spent in relation to the birth of a child or in maintaining a child can be claimed under Schedule 1 at any time, and on more than one occasion. To make the payment of the lump sum affordable for the paying parent, a judge can say that the lump sum should be paid in instalments.

You might use this provision if you have incurred credit card debts specifically in relation to your child's expenses, or where one-off expenditure is required. Examples include: buying nursery furniture, purchasing a car to transport your child, a contribution to a house purchase, necessary works on your property referable to your child's needs or buying a computer to assist your child with their homework.

Costs associated with your child's disability

If your child has a disability then Schedule 1 can be used to apply for increased periodical payments, any number of lump sum payments and provision for housing improvements or housing outright which are due to your child's disability-related needs. You will need to set out and evidence those needs and show that you have researched the costs of those needs which relate to your child's disability. An example of this might be where an extension or alterations are needed to your house to accommodate your child's disability, such as to make it wheel-chair-friendly. You will need to prove that you cannot contribute to the cost of those works alone or at all. If you think that your ex-partner has the means to cover those costs, you can consider making a claim against them under Schedule 1.

Legal fees

If you are considering making an application for a court order or if you are already in court against your ex-partner, such as in relation to a dispute over the arrangements for your children or as part of a financial claim under Schedule 1, and you cannot afford your family lawyer's legal fees to represent you in those court proceedings, you may also be able to apply under Schedule 1 for your ex-partner to pay some or all of your legal fees. A successful claim will be on the basis that it is in your children's best interests for you to have appropriate legal representation in that case and you have no other way of funding your legal fees yourself (and your ex-partner can afford it).

That latter part in brackets makes all claims under Schedule 1 quite tricky, unless your ex-partner has significant and obvious wealth. If you are considering whether to make claims or if you want to defend a potential claim, you really should do so in consultation with a family lawyer. The discretion and circumstantial differences of these types of claims means they need to be carefully considered. Further, there is a risk of having to pay the other person's legal costs if you are not successful in your claims, and that financial risk to you makes taking legal advice proportionate and necessary. There may be jurisdictional issues if one of the parents or children lives abroad and you will need a family lawyer to check any potential issues for you.

I always advise attempting to agree matters between you, but it is best to do so having had some advice from a family lawyer so that you are aware of the potential claims and limitations of any such claims under Schedule 1. If you cannot agree between you then try non-court dispute resolution methods (see Chapter 5) before starting court proceedings. There is a set process and procedure which applies to Schedule 1 claims, whereby you both fully set out your opinions and evidence and each of you disclose your financial means. It is a similar but shortened version of the process and procedure undertaken in financial disputes in divorce cases.

Changing Your Mind

Settlement terms in respect of maintenance are variable, upwards or downwards at any point during the term of its payment. Changing your mind quite soon after the initial terms were reached will not usually cut it. You and your ex-partner can agree to vary maintenance between the two of you at any time. You do not need to go back to court to do this or even document it in writing, but I recommend that you record your new agreement in an email between you to make sure you are both of the same understanding.

If you do not agree with your ex-partner to change the maintenance, as long as there has been a change of circumstances that warrants the request to vary the maintenance, a judge will be able to consider an application to the court for a formal variation.

In respect of child maintenance, it depends on whether the paying parent earns less than £156,000 gross per year as the court will not be able to deal with a variation of child maintenance issue for you if this threshold is not met. In the absence of reaching agreement with your ex-partner you will need to contact the CMS to recalculate any change in child maintenance in accordance with their set calculations. If your ex-partner earns more than £156,000 gross per year you will need the CMS to make a maximum assessment and then you can make an application to court for a variation of the 'top-up' maintenance. If you have a court order in place flowing from your divorce and it includes provision for child maintenance, you will need to check the wording of your order before making any reductions to child maintenance following a new assessment by the CMS.

PART V

FINANCIAL SEPARATION

CHAPTER 12

Unmarried Couples

T HE LAW TREATS couples who have not married very differently to those who are married on separation – you have no financial claims or responsibility to each other under matrimonial law. There is no such thing as a common-law spouse in England and Wales and you do not acquire any rights simply because you have been together for a long time. You will not be able to make any financial claims against your partner just because you are with them for a long time (it really makes no difference how long you are together). Financial claims are not acquired over time by virtue of an unmarried relationship. Any assets that you own together in your joint names will be dealt with in strict accordance with the laws that relate to those specific assets. For example, if you have a joint bank account, you are both equally entitled to the balance and both equally responsible for any overdraft debt, unless you have expressly agreed otherwise. You might have some financial claims against each other if you own property or a business together, but otherwise you have no claims for yourself. If you have children together there is financial provision available to children, which can be made in addition to any claims you might have under, for example, property law or company law (see pages 204–212).

House Ownership

Whenever you buy a property in England and Wales you have two options for how you own it, and it is important for you to establish in which way you own your property or each of your properties (you might have more than one property and hold each differently), so that you can work out what financial interest, if any, you have or might have. If you are not sure how you own your property, and rarely people can remember with confidence, you can check the property title information, such as the transfer deed or, if you signed one, a declaration of trust. If you don't have access to these documents, and, again, people rarely have them to hand, then speak to a lawyer (a conveyancing lawyer or a family lawyer) and they should be able to easily find out for you. You can access most property documents online at the Land Registry (see Resources, page 268), but they are not always easy to interpret if you are not familiar with them.

Joint tenants

The first way to hold property is to jointly own it together as joint tenants. This is where you are both named as the legal owners on the property's title with the Land Registry and the 'rule of survivorship' applies. The rule of survivorship means that when one of you dies, the property will automatically pass on to the survivor regardless of what your will or the intestacy rules say. Most people can remember whether they hold their property as joint tenants because they can remember this rule having been explained to them by their conveyancing lawyer at the time of purchase. However, you can change it at any time to the next option, so it is still worth checking the property's title register to check.

Holding the property in this way together will mean that on sale, after repayment of any outstanding mortgages or loans secured against the property, paying for your estate agent's and conveyancing lawyer's fees and any other costs of sale, any remaining money will be shared between you equally. This overrides any unequal contributions either of you have made to the property – you will each have an equal share. As a joint owner, you have equal rights of occupation, to deal with the property and the property cannot be sold without either your consent or a court order.

It is worth noting that from separation and until you sell the property, the rule of survivorship will still apply as it is linked to the property and not your relationship status. If you were to die after your separation but before your house is sold, your half-share would still automatically pass to your now ex-partner. If you want to avoid this, you will need to sever the joint tenancy, which means switching the property ownership from joint tenants to tenants in common (see page 206). You can do this without your ex-partner's agreement, although you will need to send them a formal 'Notice' to inform them of what you are doing. In conjunction with this you should also apply to the Land Registry to place a restriction against the property's title which will record your rights and prevent a sale of the property without your knowledge and consent, which is standard procedure. A conveyancing lawyer will be able to assist you in completing this straightforward task, but you may want to speak to a family lawyer who can do this for you while also giving you holistic advice about the breakdown of your relationship.

Tenants in common

The second way to hold property is where you jointly own a property as tenants in common. The difference between tenants in common and joint tenants is that you declare what percentage interest you each have in the property. You can agree to hold a property as tenants in common in equal shares, so that you each have a 50 per cent interest in the property, or unequal shares. The benefit of being tenants in common with equal shares compared to joint tenants is that you can each leave your 50 per cent to whomever you have expressed as the beneficiary in your will, or intestacy rules will apply on your death if you do not have a will. Either way, it will not automatically pass entirely to your co-owner.

Holding your financial interest in the property in unequal shares, for example, 70 per cent to one owner and 30 per cent to the other, is usually done to reflect that one person has made a higher financial contribution to the purchase of the property than the other, with the intention of preserving their higher interest. Even if you hold an unequal and lower percentage share in the property you are still a joint legal owner and have equal rights to occupy and deal with the property, such as engaging in its sale.

No legal ownership but a financial interest

This is not the ideal situation, and is often when family lawyers are engaged. This is usually where you are not a legal owner, but your ex-partner is, and you jointly lived in the property together. The financial interest in the property can, however, be held differently to the legal ownership. Even if you are not a legal owner and have not signed any legal documents, you *may* have a case to say that the financial interest is held in part for you 'on trust'.

There are differing ways in which a beneficial interest in a property can be acquired. The starting scenario is usually where a property is purchased or had been purchased prior to the relationship in one partner's sole name. Then, during the relationship, the non-owning partner puts money into the property, such as by paying for or towards a new bathroom, an extension, or even by paying down some money on the mortgage.

If the owning partner does things properly, they will formally express in writing that a trust has been established by the non-owning partner putting money into their property and that they (the legal owner) now hold that money or a percentage share of the property 'on trust' for the non-owning partner. This is an 'express' trust and, when the property is later sold, the non-owning partner will receive a set figure or a set percentage share of the sale proceeds.

The alternatives to an express trust are harder to establish and it is in these situations that most disputes arise. The next level down from an express trust is to show that you put money in or did something which added value to the property, or that you did something to your detriment on the reliance of you and your ex-partner having a 'common intention' that you would gain a financial interest in the property. This needs to be more than just paying towards the bills for living there, and you will need to show that not only did you make the contribution or act to your detriment, but that you both had the understanding that it would give you a financial interest in the property. Common intention is often evidenced by emails/texts between you, your own recollection and/or a witness's recollection of your agreement that if you put the money into the property or did something to add value to it, in return you would have a financial interest in the property. An example of this is the owning partner saying, 'If you pay for the new kitchen you will get your money back when the property is sold'. This is a resulting trust because it is 'as a result' of either:

1. your contribution and your common intention; or
2. your act to your detriment (such as utilising your skills to put in a new kitchen) and your common intention, known as a 'constructive trust'.

The final option is to show that you relied upon the owning partner's conduct, words of assurance and promises, such as 'This is your home as much as it is mine', referring to the house as 'our property' or saying such things as 'You don't need to worry about finances, you will be looked after when we sell our house', and in addition you have done an act to your detriment because of the words and conduct of the owning partner. Examples of this are spending money, time and effort to redecorate, or reducing working hours (and therefore losing income) to project manage an extension being built. Your recollection of events alone will not be sufficient to establish an interest in the property through this route, known as 'proprietary estoppel'. You will need evidence such as photographs, bank statements, copies of emails/text messages with your ex-partner or third parties, such as suppliers, invoices and bank or credit card statements.

In the absence of any formal recording, legally or informally between you, setting out exactly what your intentions were for the property you live in together, you will need the assistance of a family lawyer to work through whether you can establish a financial interest in the property another way. Due to the complex manner of these types of cases I recommend taking legal advice early on. Once you have that advice and have gathered your evidence, you can try to reach an agreement with your ex-partner between you, but with the confidence of the knowledge your family lawyer has given you about your position in law. If that does not work then you should try a non-court dispute resolution method (see Chapter 5). If you still cannot reach a settlement between you, an application to the court will need to be made, but the process is different to matrimonial cases and I recommend engaging a family lawyer to assist you with this.

Other Financial Ties

Businesses

If you have a business together you will need to review the documents that were produced when the company was set up or since, such as the shareholders' agreement, to figure out what your interest is in the business and how you can retrieve your interest, if that is what you want to do. It might be that there is no formal recording of you having a financial interest in the business. If you are unclear or think that any subsequent actions or discussions might have changed your initial arrangements then you will need to seek legal advice. In these situations, a family lawyer can review your situation and potential claims against your ex-partner as a whole, but they will also probably need to work with a corporate lawyer, so try to choose one that has such a connection.

Just because your personal relationship has changed status, does not mean that you and your ex-partner cannot continue with your business relationship. However, if you find it too difficult to continue to work together you will need to figure out a way to separate your work and your financial interest (if any). This can be difficult as you do not want to rock the business which is usually the hand that feeds the family. It is also possible that you may need advice from an accountant to discuss the best way for your business separation to work financially for you both.

Bank accounts and investments

If you have bank accounts or investments together in your joint names, you are both equally entitled to the funds in those accounts. This is regardless of whether you contributed unequally towards the funds, unless you have something to show that you agreed otherwise, such as emails or messages between you documenting your alternative agreement or a cohabitation agreement (which is like a nuptial agreement for the unmarried). You should both have access to those accounts, even if immediate access to the funds is not possible by virtue of the account's investment restrictions. If you fear that your ex-partner might empty some of or the whole account you can consider whether it might be appropriate for you to put a restriction on your account to prevent sole withdrawals or transfers, and perhaps even transfer your half-share into an account in your sole name. If your accounts are offshore or of significant sums, you should take financial advice before doing so in case there are any tax consequences or penalties to pay. Be warned that taking money out of joint accounts will not go down well with your ex-partner. It will heighten tensions and could be a catalyst to other unilateral actions. It is best to discuss first what it is that you think should happen before either of you takes any action.

Cars

Assets such as cars can only be legally owned in one person's name. It is common for one partner to be the legal owner but for the other partner to be the main driver. In which case, on separation, there is often a dispute over the car. If common sense and direct talks cannot prevail with a sensible outcome, you may need a family lawyer to write to your ex-partner on your behalf with your proposal to settle the dispute. This type of issue is often resolved by a lawyer's letter.

Remember that if you have a child together you can make claims under Schedule 1 for lump sums relating to your child's needs (see page 194). If a car is necessary to your care of your child, such as needing the car to take your child to and from school, then you should either seek an agreement for the car to be transferred to your sole name or, if it cannot be agreed that you can keep the car, you will need to consider whether you should make a claim under Schedule 1 for a lump sum from your ex-partner to enable you to purchase a car (either for a deposit or for the full amount).

Pets

Similar to cars, pets can only be registered in one person's name, but this does not reflect that often the pet belongs emotionally to both ex-partners. A family pet can be a much-fought-over asset and it can be difficult to resolve such a dispute because pets are often thought of as equal to a child of the family and emotions can run high. Ideally, the pet would be better staying with one person post-separation, but I have experienced situations where I have drawn up an agreement, similar to a child arrangements order, setting out who the pet will live with and when, so that the pet shares its time between the ex-partners, and to include how the pet's expenses should be shared between them.

My advice is to be sensible and keep the dispute in perspective and proportionate to your means of funding that dispute if you decide to involve a family lawyer.

Personal belongings and house contents

Unless you can show that a particular item was inherited by you, gifted to you or purchased by you to warrant you claiming its ownership, it is difficult to say who owns what. Usually, ex-partners simply agree to work together on dividing up their personal belongings and house contents. If you get on well you could walk around your house together and discuss who will keep what, or you could make a list of the items you specifically want to keep and send it to your ex-partner for them to agree. If you jointly purchased items, you will need to work together to agree who will keep them if they can't be divided, such as a sofa, but try to do so in a compensatory manner, such as 'I'll keep the sofas and you can keep the dining table and chairs.'

Resolving financial issues at the end of an unmarried relationship can be just as difficult to unravel as a married one if you own a property together and it is not clear who has contributed what. For those who have a record of financial contributions, the unravelling can be far clearer cut, and therefore there is the potential for a less acrimonious financial separation. The law is not as generous with unmarried couples' financial claims as it is with separating spouses, and it tends to lead to disappointment, particularly after a long cohabiting relationship or where there are children. Remember, your children's financial claims are separate to your own, and you should remind yourself of Chapter 11 about what financial provision might be available for them.

CHAPTER 13

Married Couples/Civil Partners

I F YOU HAVE decided to divorce and one of you has started divorce proceedings, either of you (it does not need to be the same spouse who applied for the divorce) can make an application to the court for a financial order to be made to separate your finances. The financial proceedings are referred to as 'financial remedy proceedings'. In most cases people agree that they will divorce and then try to separate their finances without an application being made to the court. It is usual that people discuss the options between them, or they use a non-court dispute resolution method, commonly using mediation or family lawyers to negotiate on their behalf (see Chapter 5). Financial separation can be achieved without having to battle about it through the courts. Court should always be a last resort.

It is important for you to try to separate your finances upon divorce to enable you to both move on with clarity and independence of each other. The ideal situation is that you reach a settlement whereby you have no ongoing financial ties between you, but this is rarely achieved as there tends to be a need for future ongoing responsibilities, such as a later house sale in years to come or the ongoing payment of spousal and/ or child maintenance. Whether or not there are to be ongoing financial ties between you, it is best for those terms to be set and the boundaries put in place so that you can move forward with your lives with the security of knowing what is yours now and in the future.

You do not need to separate and divorce immediately, and many clients have asked me whether they need to rush into a divorce. It is not for me to tell anybody whether they should get a divorce, but for those who have decided they want a divorce, my advice is that there is usually little point in prolonging the inevitable because of the financial consequences. Those who make assumptions about continuing financial support or reach an informal agreement, often find themselves (and sometimes quite quickly) in dispute because their spouse wants to change the agreement, suddenly stops paying for something they had previously paid for or withdraws money from an account without joint consent. It is much better to separate with clear boundaries about who will have what and who will continue to pay for what.

Joint Finances

As long as you and your spouse agree, you can decide when to do things such as close or transfer joint bank accounts, divide up your personal belongings and even put your house on the market for sale. If you are not sure if it is the right thing to do, speak to a family lawyer before you do it as it's either impossible or very difficult to undo once you have done it.

Usually couples have at least one joint bank account which has the direct debits for the mortgage or rent, utility bills and household expenses. Sometimes it's also the main account for all the family's expenditure. If you have just separated then remember my advice is to, where possible, maintain the status quo, which means you each continue to contribute as before your separation. It usually makes sense for you to continue to use your joint account, with all the direct debits set up, as you did previously. If you are amicable, it is a matter of discussing this and agreeing what you will each continue to pay in, and what is agreed can be taken out. If the joint account is also used for day-to-day spending, such as grocery shops, entertainment and clothing, you should clarify whether 'maintaining the status quo' includes that kind of expenditure too. In my view it should, but if money is tight because it is now being stretched across two households, then perhaps some economies need to be made by both of you, and you will need to discuss what spending should be prioritised and what needs to be cut back.

If you are not amicable then it is likely to become a bit of a flashpoint for you to have this type of discussion. See if you can switch up how you communicate with each other to make this conversation possible by another means, such as via emails instead of face-to-face (see Chapter 4). Itemise the expenditure you think should continue to be met and which you think could be reduced, if necessary. Make sure you are clear about what needs to be transferred into the account every month and by whom. It is very common in a fraught situation for one spouse to decide to stop their salary being paid into the joint account, or to stop or dramatically reduce their usual monthly transfers in. This is an indication of the 'It's my money and we're separated now so I don't have to give you anything' mindset. This is wrong and if you are tempted to do this, please don't. If you find yourself the recipient of such a move then contact a family lawyer if you are unable to convince your spouse to correct their actions.

Spouses have potential claims against each other, and those claims are available as soon as you separate if there is an urgent need. If you find yourself cut off or in urgent financial need while trying to negotiate and settle your overall financial separation, you can make a claim for interim maintenance and even interim lump sums of money. You will need to show that you do not have income or assets of your own sufficient to meet your urgent needs, and that you have good reason to believe that your spouse can afford it. Interim claims are considered as basic and essential needs, but what is essential expenditure for you will depend on the standard of living you enjoyed during the marriage. A holiday, for example, is usually considered a luxury and not included as part of an interim need. Basic and essential needs include outgoings such as (but not limited to) your mortgage or rent, utilities, food, essential clothing, transportation costs, necessary health expenses, work-related expenditure, and the same for your children to include any necessary educational expenses. Interim claims are common, although they can be difficult to make. You will need to make sure you have done what you can to mitigate your own situation, such as reviewing your entitlement to state benefits, making reasonable economies to your outgoings and potentially even taking a job or increasing your working hours.

It is rare that amicable couples find themselves in a situation where interim claims are being made against each other, because sensible communication takes place where they openly discuss what they each need and they reasonably figure out how those needs can be met while the bigger picture gets sorted out. Where there are disputes between couples, unreasonable actions by one or both spouses can quickly lead to poor relations, bad communication (if any at all) and financial difficulties. A higher-earning spouse will be ill-advised to simply cut off or unreasonably reduce their spouse's access to money as it will result in their spouse having to make interim claims, and incur the legal costs of doing so, which only reduces the marital pot of money.

If you are unreasonably preventing your spouse from accessing funds they need and, as so often happens, as a result they are forced to take out a loan, they will have to factor in that loan and the interest it attracts as part of their financial needs in the overall financial settlement. Any unreasonable actions are likely to cause a further depletion of matrimonial funds available for division between you because debts attract interest and legal costs to force an unreasonable spouse to behave reasonably. If there is no other incentive to be reasonable, it is that it has the potential to reduce what you receive in the overall settlement.

If relations are not great with your spouse and you fear that they might unreasonably make withdrawals from any of your joint bank accounts, savings accounts or investments, you can consider whether it is appropriate to contact your provider(s) and ask them to put a restriction against your account which prevents any withdrawals being made without joint consent. This works well for a savings account, where you both retain equal access and the asset is transparent to both of you, and you both have the security of knowing that the other cannot simply empty the account. Any such behaviour like this is only going to heighten the tension between you and make negotiating a settlement more difficult, time-consuming and potentially more expensive.

A court cannot make an interim order (while your overall settlement is settled) for a house to be sold, so if spouses cannot agree whether a property should be sold you will not be able to force the issue until the final stage of the court process. If you and your spouse agree that your house needs to be put on the market for sale then you can. A solely owning spouse should be wary of thinking that they can put the house on the market for sale because they are the sole legal owner. An occupying spouse has rights of occupation and would be well-advised to enter a matrimonial home rights notice against the Land Registry property title to register those rights. This notice highlights the rights of occupation to a potential buyer and gives some protection that the house cannot be sold without the occupier's knowledge. If you have concerns about other assets in your spouse's sole name being sold without your consent or knowledge, you should urgently discuss ways in which those assets might be preserved with a family lawyer. Court intervention for emergency remedies is usually only proportionate in bigger money cases, but a letter from your family lawyer might be a good alternative for those who are not millionaires.

Before you agree to put your house on the market for sale you should first discuss its sale as part of your overall potential claims with a family lawyer. The caution is that it is rarely possible to deal with your financial separation in a piecemeal manner, meaning taking assets in isolation and dealing with them without reference to the overall settlement. A family lawyer will also talk you through the practicalities of the sale, to include how the sale should be conducted and what should be done with the sale proceeds on completion. If you have not decided the overall settlement, how can you each agree on what to do with the sale proceeds?

My best advice for an interim situation while you work out your overall financial separation is to hold the pre-separation position where possible. If this is not possible, try to be reasonable. Remember that the impact of any unreasonable or unilateral behaviour is not just financial; it will no doubt cause animosity and make it harder to reach agreement on your overall settlement. If you have children together, it also has the potential to impact upon their well-being and your ongoing co-parenting relationship.

The detail of your financial unravelling, such as the transfer or closing of joint accounts, switching of direct debits, dividing up contents, transferring assets or paying off debts, can be done as part of your final settlement and is normally detailed in your court order. Fear of dealing with these matters in the interim is often because full and frank financial disclosure is yet to be exchanged or the overall settlement terms are not yet agreed. When in this interim position of uncertainty, it is difficult to make such practical progress without worrying that you might be prejudicing your overall case, or that your spouse is encouraging you to do something out of self-interest for them. Trust is not always at its highest at this point of a divorce and you might be dealing with things at a different pace. One spouse might have wanted a divorce for a while and so mentally is further ahead with coping with these practical separations compared to the other spouse. Communication with your spouse will make a difference, but if it is not reasonable then communication with a family lawyer will probably be necessary.

How to Separate Your Finances

It is probably worthwhile explaining that the jurisdiction of England and Wales is known as the 'divorce capital of the world' because our laws about how to separate finances on divorce are wide-reaching and discretionary, so people are often attracted to apply these laws to their financial settlement on divorce in the hope that they will apply favourably to them. There is a set structure in written law about what should be considered in deciding how a couple's finances should be separated. To interpret those laws, the outcomes of previous court cases, known as 'case law', are also considered to understand how the written law should be applied.

There is no set formula, but that means that there will be more than one interpretation of how considerations should be weighted in any given case. Due to the flexibility of our laws, there is usually a range of what would be a reasonable settlement, meaning there is not just one correct outcome. Discussions about how to separate your finances can therefore be prime for dispute, but it does not necessarily mean that either of you is in the wrong; it comes down to how each of you is interpreting and applying the law.

In conjunction with understanding the law and how it might apply to you, you need to also apply common sense. Our laws are wide-reaching, which means that, for most situations, a transfer of an asset or responsibility for a debt can be transferred from one spouse to another as part of the settlement. It does not matter who has what in their sole name – this does not protect that asset from division with your spouse on divorce as matrimonial laws can override legal ownership. However, this does mean that when talking about how to separate your finances you can be quite creative in how to make it work for you, and common sense should be a vital part of that.

The ability to apply the law to your circumstances is the art of the family lawyer, using their knowledge of the written law and case law to finely balance the application of those laws to you. While some couples are able to reach a financial settlement between them, if you are in dispute or have any complexities to your circumstances I would recommend taking the advice of a family lawyer to get an informed indication of the bracket within which your reasonable settlement might lie. You can then use this information to give you confidence in negotiating your settlement yourself or, if that is not possible, in using a non-court dispute resolution method, such as mediation or solicitors' negotiations (see Chapter 5).

What you should do first

It is quite common for clients to tell me that they don't know much about their own financial position let alone their spouse's finances. Before you can discuss your financial separation, you must get yourself up to date about your own finances and be informed about your spouse's. Even if you think you can agree a financial settlement with your spouse, you cannot reach a fair settlement without full knowledge of what both of you have available for division. Both spouses must set out fully their financial positions and the talks and negotiations can flow from there. However, it is common for a spouse to feel unsure about what has been disclosed and whether there is anything missing, the suggestion being that their spouse has not been completely honest. Being open and honest is not only a prerequisite to a good financial separation, it is an obligation. If trust is an issue, it makes the amicability of the process very difficult.

When I refer to your 'financial position' I mean everything and anything to do with your finances. Below is a list of things to help you think about what you will need to disclose and what will be considered as part of achieving a fair settlement:

- Your health, and that of your children.
- Any existing agreements for maintenance to be paid either by you to someone, or received by you from your spouse or a previous partner.
- The possible, or preferably agreed, arrangements for how your children will spend their time between you.
- Property, whether you own it in your sole name or your joint name with your spouse or someone else. This includes where you do not have a property in your legal name but you have an agreement with the legal owner that you have a financial interest in that property. You need to disclose as part of your property interest information about any mortgages or loans against the property, other people's interests in the property, the amount outstanding on any such liabilities and their fees for repayment (such as an early redemption fee or administration fees), and estimate how much it would cost to sell the property if you were to release your interest and the proportion of those costs for which you would be liable (usually in proportion to your percentage of ownership).
- Bank accounts and savings accounts.
- Investments such as ISAs, shareholdings, premium bonds, etc.
- Life insurance policies including endowment policies, even if they do not have a cash value.
- Any money owed to you, such as money you have lent to someone, but also to include money paid out but due back to you, for example, a rental deposit.

- Cash (of more than £500) that you have which is not in a bank account or investment.
- Personal belongings that are individually worth more than £500. The value attributable to such belongings should be what you would get if you were to sell that item in its current condition on a second-hand market, not what you paid for it and not its insurance value. Examples include jewellery, cars or antiques.
- Debts, to include credit cards, formal loans (from a bank or other professional lender) or informal loans (from a friend or family member) and hire purchase agreements (such as for a car).
- Any liability you might have to pay tax on if you were to sell any of your assets, such as capital gains tax, or if you were to bring foreign monies onshore to England and Wales.
- Business interests.
- Pensions. You will need to specifically ask each pension provider to give you what is called a 'cash equivalent' valuation of your fund, meaning a cash figure to represent what your pension pot is currently worth.
- If you are a beneficiary or potential beneficiary of a trust fund.
- Your potential finances for the foreseeable future, such as a one-off bonus, inheritance or an expected gift.
- Income from all sources to include employment, self-employment, interest earned on investments, rental income, dividends and state benefits.
- Your estimated itemised annual expenditure for you and, if applicable, your children (this will later be referenced as your 'income needs').

- Your estimated capital requirements, being the capital you think you need to spend to meet your housing needs, and other capital expenses such as a car, home improvements and retraining. I have even had a client who required breast implant replacements every 10 years who included the cost of those replacements as part of her capital needs.

It is important to know that your disclosure of your financial position is not limited to what you have or owe just in England and Wales. You must also include international assets, income and debts, for example:

- Foreign earnings or income from foreign investments or rental income from a foreign property, such as a holiday home.
- Owning a holiday home.
- Having an interest in an offshore trust fund.
- If you lived abroad and have a bank account left open in that country.
- If you paid into a pension fund, for example, via your employment while you lived abroad.
- Foreign tax liability, such as on the sale of a holiday home or from your foreign income.

Full disclosure means everything from everywhere.

Telling your spouse verbally or in an email about your financial position will not normally be sufficient. You should not only inform them of everything about your finances, you should also exchange documents to evidence your financial position. The court-required standard of financial disclosure is a good measurement, and I refer to this standard as a benchmark, not because your case will necessarily end up being disputed through the courts, but because it ensures you are both completing and exchanging your disclosure at the same standard. The court requires both spouses to complete and exchange their financial disclosure using a form called a 'Form E'. This is accessible and available on the government website (https://www.gov.uk/), even if you are not currently engaged in court proceedings. The form helps you to make sure you have listed and explained all the above stated elements of your financial position, and more helpfully sets out exactly which documents you must disclose to evidence each of those points. For example, for each bank account you hold in your sole name or in your joint name, you must disclose 12 months' statements. If you are not in the court process and you trust that your spouse is giving you full and frank disclosure, you might agree to provide disclosure to a less onerous degree.

Providing each other with your financial disclosure without being in court proceedings is referred to as 'voluntary disclosure' and, even on a voluntary basis, I recommend that it is done with the assistance of a family lawyer. This is because your financial position is not only the black-and-white facts of your house value, bank balances and debts, but also the narrative around how you got to that financial position. This narrative includes when you acquired assets or liabilities, the reason behind why you acquired them and how, as well as discussions you and your spouse have had about your respective financial positions and any agreements you might have made along the way, either informally between you or more formally, such as in a prenuptial agreement, postnuptial agreement or declaration of trust. This financial narrative might influence the outcome of your financial settlement, so it is important to take advice to ensure that your whole financial position is provided and appropriately set out.

Providing each other with your financial disclosure and evidence in isolation will not necessarily enable you to discuss your financial separation as it is rare that you will both have the same expectations of how your finances should be divided between you. This is where an understanding of the law is necessary for you to have enough confidence to engage in talks with your spouse about what a reasonable and fair settlement might be.

What the law says

The written law is set out in Section 25 of the Matrimonial Causes Act 1973. This sets the guidelines for how financial settlements should be considered, and these are referred to as the 'Section 25 Factors' (and are similarly set out in the Civil Partnership Act 2004 in respect of civil partners). For ease of reference, and not wishing to cause any offence, I shall refer to spouses, marriage and divorce to include civil partners, civil partnership and dissolution of a civil partnership.

The law states that the starting point for deciding how to separate finances on divorce is to consider certain factors of the marriage. They are not listed in any priority and they will each carry different weight depending on your specific circumstances. The Section 25 Factors are:

- The income, earning capacity, property and other financial resources that each of you have or are likely to have in the foreseeable future, including in the case of earning capacity any increase in that capacity which it would in the opinion of the court be reasonable to expect a party to the marriage to take steps to acquire.

- The financial needs, obligations and responsibilities that each of you have or are likely to have in the foreseeable future.
- The standard of living enjoyed by the family before separation.
- The age of the spouses and the length of the marriage.
- Any physical or mental disability of either spouse.
- The contributions that each spouse has made or is likely in the foreseeable future to make to the welfare of the family, including any contribution by looking after the home or caring for the family.
- The conduct of each spouse, if that conduct is such that it would, in the opinion of the court, be inequitable to disregard it.
- The value to each spouse of any benefit which, by reason of the dissolution or annulment of the marriage, that party will lose the chance of acquiring.

All of these factors must be balanced against each other in determining who should get what as part of your financial settlement. As spouses, you have three types of financial claim against each other: they are in respect of capital (for example, your house, savings and investments), income (from all sources) and pension. The ideal situation is where neither of you has any future financial ties to the other – this is known as a 'clean break'. If you cannot achieve a clean break in respect of all three claims against each other, it is possible to have a clean break in respect of, for example, pension only but with ongoing ties for a specified or unspecified period in respect of capital and income.

Being financially independent of each other means that you each walk away solely reliant on your own financial resources and income. It is not always possible to achieve this. For example, one spouse may not be able to be self-sufficient on their income alone and so they require some maintenance to meet their outgoings. This would mean that a clean break is unlikely to be achieved in respect of income. You will need to agree a term, if possible, for how long you will be financially tied. All of this will be considered as part of the balancing consideration of the Section 25 Factors and their interpretation and application to your case in light of case law. The principle of fairness is placed firmly at the centre of interpretation and the starting point is equality. With the starting point of equality in mind you need to think about whether an equal division of your finances between you would be a fair outcome when considering all the Section 25 Factors.

What is meant by 'fair' has been tested by other people's cases and it has been established that fairness should be considered in respect of both spouses and any children's needs, with the children's needs being placed as a priority above either of the spouses' own needs. To work out what your needs are you will need to consider what you and, if you have any, your children need to provide you with a home and to sustain your lifestyle (your capital needs, such as a house, car, savings for a rainy day, etc.), money each month to pay your outgoings and responsibilities (your income needs), and provision for your retirement (your pension needs). You must be reasonable in your expectations and the word 'reasonable' features a lot in deciding how to fairly divide your finances.

Capital Needs

Housing

For most cases, each spouse's needs, or where there are any children, the children's needs, determine the outcome, and creativity combined with common sense enable that to happen.

If you have children you will need to have an idea, if not an agreement, about what the arrangements will be for them to spend time with you both post-separation. If it is likely that they will spend time overnight with you both, then both parents will have a need for a home with enough bedrooms for themselves and the children to stay overnight, even if their time is spent unequally between them. It is often the case that there is insufficient capital for both of you to immediately afford to buy two properties, and this is where you need to think reasonably, creatively and with common sense. The priority is for your children to have a secure roof over their heads, and the money will therefore need to be placed in favour of the parent with whom the children live for most of their time.

Simply allowing one spouse to have all the capital may not seem fair when considering all the Section 25 Factors in your case, but it must be balanced against your children's needs as they are the priority. If there is enough money for one spouse to retain the former matrimonial home, or for a property to be purchased sufficient to meet one spouse's and your children's reasonable needs, that is often the preferred situation over both spouses each being in rented accommodation, which offers less security for the children's home. Usually, where the capital is heavily weighted towards one spouse in order to prioritise the children, there is provision for the other spouse to receive a fair share of that capital in the future, when the children reach an older age and the spouse is able to increase their earnings and/or downsize.

Each of your mortgage capacities should be considered as part of the available capital provision, and the allocation of any capital either in existing property or savings should be considered alongside your respective mortgage capacities. Is it possible for you to each have some capital and use your mortgage capacities to provide you each with an owned home, albeit subject to a mortgage? There are some mortgage providers who will consider, as part of a spouse's mortgage capacity and affordability, money they receive by way of spousal maintenance and/or child maintenance if it is set out in a court order (a court order should be obtained in any event upon your settlement of your finances, so this should not be an issue).

An example of this working is where there is an existing property, usually the former matrimonial home, in which one spouse and their children will continue to live, and the spouse who is to live there can obtain a mortgage in their sole name considering their earnings, maintenance and state benefits, if applicable. This has the benefit of releasing the other spouse from that property's mortgage, achieving a capital clean break between them and enabling the other spouse to keep their own mortgage capacity available for them to use to meet their housing needs, either immediately or in the future once they have saved up some capital for a deposit.

Other options include you both being joint owners of a property, often with a joint mortgage, but with the agreement in place now for a division of the sale proceeds between you when the property will be sold in the future. This type of postponed sale of a property means your children's housing needs are met and prioritised, and the non-resident spouse retains an investment in that property knowing that, upon a set event in the future, the house will be sold and their share of the capital will be released to them.

You should agree now what your respective shares in that property will be, for example 50/50, an unequal percentage split or a set amount of money if not a percentage. The later date for sale is usually set out as 'the first to occur of' a number of trigger events which will happen in the future. Where the property is being used to provide children with a home it is often connected with their education milestones, such as the youngest child finishing their secondary school education, but you can agree any date or event that works in both of your circumstances. Other triggering events can include your ex-spouse's cohabitation (although this is often disputed), remarriage, death or a further court order for the property to be sold. Upon the first of the triggering events to occur the residing spouse would normally have the option to buy out the other spouse, or the property will be sold and provisions for how the property will be sold are set out as part of the settlement now to avoid any later disputes.

If you do not have any children's needs to consider, a starting position of an equal division is likely to be more closely kept, but must be balanced against all of the Section 25 Factors. Are there any other reasons why either of you should receive more capital than the other? Considerations such as a short length of marriage and assets acquired prior to that marriage will be quite powerful in arguing away from an equal division of the capital. A guiding rule for a short marriage where there are no children tends to be that you each take away what you brought in, and any capital accrued during the marriage might be divided equally (if that would be sufficient to meet needs). This type of discretionary application of the law is why issues become disputed and guidance from a family lawyer is so important for assessing whether your expectations are reasonable and therefore worth pursuing further.

Debts

Your capital needs are not just related to your housing, and it is common that they also refer to your need to meet your debts. If debts form a significant part of your financial position and there is insufficient capital to prioritise housing needs and repay debts, you will need to consider all your options. An example is whether it would be possible to consolidate debts and lower the monthly repayments to free up some income, which would then improve mortgage capacity and affordability, or even make renting a more suitable home achievable.

Cars and other capital requirements

Your other capital needs that are commonly considered include things like whether you need a car or to replace your existing one, do any works to your property, such as a new bathroom or upgrade your boiler, pay tax (such as stamp duty land tax on the purchase of a property) or have money available to undertake courses to enable you to retrain to get a better job or return to the workplace. You should also set out any capital expenditure required for your children, such as a new computer for their homework or larger one-off expenses like driving lessons and a car for their use.

The hardest cases to settle are those with limited funds because there are insufficient monies to meet both spouses' needs without one or both spouses feeling like the settlement is unfair. There are two key ways for you to cope with this. The first is by setting your expectations reasonably from the start, and you can only really do that by taking advice from a family lawyer. The second is by being flexible and creative about how you can make the financial plan work for you both, and again a family lawyer, and perhaps an accountant if proportionate, will be able to think through alternative options with you and how to make a fair settlement workable.

Whatever the arrangement is for your capital settlement, it is not variable once finalised (although there are rare exceptions). This means that even if you are making arrangements for a future sale of property and division of the capital at a later date, neither of you will be able to change your minds. Capital settlements are made once and for all.

Income Needs

How to calculate your income needs

To calculate your income needs, you really need to have an idea of what you want to happen in respect of your capital needs. The reason you need to think about your capital settlement first is so that you can include such things as your rent or mortgage repayments, utility bills and associated expenses based on the kind of property you think you will live in within your budget. You will need to estimate what you each think your expenditure will be on average over a year, taking into account everything you spend money on (for you and your children) to give you your annual expenditure budget. To make it more manageable, divide the annual figure by 12 and it will give you your monthly income needs, meaning how much you will need each month to meet your reasonable expenditure requirements.

Remember that this is not a wish list; it is an estimate, as accurate as possible, with reflection on your historic spending and in anticipation of your future affordability, of what you might reasonably spend. For most separating spouses, the standard of living enjoyed during the marriage will not be affordable now that the same level of income needs to stretch across two homes, and so economies will have to be made by both of you going forward, such as less expensive cars, lowering spending on clothing, eating out, and reducing spending on entertainment and holidays. It is always a cause of conflict when, post-separation, one spouse feels like they are consciously making economies while their spouse continues to enjoy luxuries such as takeaways, nights out and holidays.

This point goes back to my advice about the importance of trying to keep things amicable because of its potential to impact upon your financial settlement. It makes it much easier for you to fall out during the process if one or both of you are behaving in a way which you know will upset the other, and seeing on your spouse's bank statements (provided to you as part of your exchange of financial disclosure) that they are spending money when you are consciously not, definitely causes conflict. Another flashpoint for upset is seeing on your spouse's disclosure payments for things such as online dating websites or spending with a new partner.

Mitigating your income needs

You will need to think about your income and whether it is appropriate in your new circumstances for you to do anything to increase it. One option is to always check whether, once you have physically separated, you will now be eligible for state benefits or an increase in your existing benefits. Remember also that if you live alone (including if you live with your children) you will qualify for a single person's discount on your council tax bill, so it is worth informing your Local Authority of your new status.

In situations where, during the marriage, it was agreed that one spouse would not work or would only work part-time in order to look after the children, pressure is often put on that spouse to either return to work or increase their working hours post-separation. If you have children, you will need to think about whether doing so would be in their best interests, or proportionate if you then have to pay for childcare. Your increased earnings might be countered by the costs of childcare. If one spouse is to return to work, you should factor in the time it will take them to retrain or gain appropriate work experience, the cost of retraining (and this can form part of that spouse's capital needs) and time to find a job and build up earnings, as it may not be reasonable to expect that spouse to walk straight into a well-paid and flexible job.

EARNING CAPACITY

It is common for one spouse to say that their job is at risk of redundancy or a salary reduction, that they want to switch jobs to something less pressured and lower earning, or that their bonus will no longer be paid. The cynic might view these claims as someone wanting to avoid or at least limit the financial claims made by their spouse against them. Such claims tend to cause panic in their spouse. If someone is genuinely at risk of redundancy they will need to evidence it by producing copies of correspondence from the employer informing them of their risk of redundancy and updates throughout the redundancy process. Even so, it may be likely that, upon redundancy, they would be able to find alternative employment at a similar level of earning. Where a spouse is casting doubt over their future earnings, it is sensible to consider that spouse's record of earnings over the last few years, and any other external (and evidenced) factors that might influence a change in that, such as a change in their health or a change in the industry they work in.

For example, when the credit crunch hit in 2007 there were a lot of people in the finance industry out of work and genuinely unable to immediately find similar employment. Also, a spouse who has suffered a heart attack, for example, might understandably be advised not to return to a high-pressured job. There are, of course, reasonable exceptions, but otherwise a spouse will be considered to have an ability to earn a certain amount of salary, known as an 'earning capacity, when considering their previous level of earning and reasonable potential to maintain that or improve it. A simple wish to have a change of career for something much lower paid is unlikely to be achievable in most cases, as, despite the divorce, you each have financial responsibilities that must be met.

Assessing affordability and requirement for maintenance

Once you have an idea of your likely future income (from all sources) and your respective income needs, you can calculate whether you have an estimated monthly surplus or deficit. The amount by which you have a deficit is how you quantify your need for maintenance from your spouse. You can evidence and explain to your spouse what you need the money for and that you are unable to meet those needs from your own income sources. However, it needs to be considered in the balance of your spouse's income and affordability to meet your deficit in addition to their own income needs.

Remember that there is a set formula for how to calculate a liability for child maintenance (see page 188). If you are the parent who will receive the child maintenance, you should include your receipt of child maintenance as it will be paid to you regardless of your income needs (because it is not calculated in reference to your expenditure), and must be included as part of your income sources when looking at whether you have a deficit between your income and outgoings. If you still have a deficit then you have a potential need for spousal maintenance, which can be paid in addition to child maintenance. Spousal maintenance and child maintenance are separate and distinct, even if some of your deficit is incurred by expenditure on your children.

HOW LONG SHOULD MAINTENANCE BE PAID FOR?

Once you have quantified how much you need by way of spousal maintenance you need to consider for how long it is reasonable for that amount of spousal maintenance to continue to be paid to you. The ideal situation is that you are financially independent of each other as quickly as possible, and so it is rare that spousal maintenance would be paid until the end of your life. It is increasingly common for spousal maintenance to be paid for a set number of years, contingent upon a future event occurring which it is anticipated will enable you to be financially independent of your ex-spouse. For many, this is difficult to predict. The test for a clean break for spousal maintenance is whether it can be achieved without the receiving spouse incurring undue hardship. Future trigger events for a decrease or 'step down' in spousal maintenance payments, or for it to be brought to a complete end, can include events such as:

- children reaching a certain age and stage of schooling, whereby it would be possible for the receiving spouse to increase their working hours and therefore their income to replace the maintenance need
- the receiving spouse's remarriage or cohabitation for more than a set period of time
- the death of either spouse
- a later court order

The terms of your settlement for maintenance are variable even after you have reached a settlement and had it set out in a court order. At any point during the term you and your spouse can agree to either increase or decrease the amount of maintenance paid and/or the term for how long it is paid (unless this extension possibility is excluded as part of your settlement). You can also agree future variations, such as an annual increase in line with inflation or a future reduction (often referred to as a 'step down') at a particular point in time. However, usually these changes are limited to an unanticipated significant event happening that has an impact upon either the receiving or paying parent, such as a child being sick and requiring the receiving parent to have to reduce their working hours to meet their care needs or the receiving parent becoming involuntarily redundant and without sufficient income, in which case they ask the paying parent to increase their maintenance. In addition, the paying parent's income could, out of their control, be significantly reduced to the extent that they cannot reasonably continue to pay spousal maintenance. Such variations must be done either by agreement or a further court order. A paying parent cannot simply stop paying on their own accord – this would be a breach of a court order.

Pension Needs

Your pension need will be mainly dependent upon what pension provision is available between you for division and how close you both are to retirement. The closer you each are to retirement, the higher your need for pension provision. In a situation where there is a disparity in spouses' careers and earnings it is common for one spouse to have a greater pension fund than the other. There are a few options available to divide pension assets between spouses, but the most common is where one spouse receives a transfer of a percentage of their spouse's pension fund into a pension fund in their own name. The mechanism available to make such a transfer is a called a 'pension sharing order'.

Remember that even if you settle your financial separation without going through court, you will need to turn those settlement terms into a consent order and that is how you will obtain the vital pension sharing order, which your pension provider will use to implement the transfer, after which it cannot be varied so neither of you can later try to change your pension settlement.

The division of pension assets is different to dividing up capital as, although you are given a 'cash equivalent' valuation of your various funds, it is not the same as having cash in the bank. A pension fund is built up to provide you with an income upon retirement, and so it is not a matter of balancing the cash equivalent value of the funds between you, but instead dividing up the potential income that might later be produced. Pensions are subject to tax, which may differ between spouses depending on your individual tax thresholds. As they are different types of assets, one pound of a pension fund does not necessarily translate to one pound of cash in the bank.

Statistics form part of calculating how to determine each spouse's pension needs and as a female has a longer life expectancy than a male, her pension fund will need to provide her with an income for longer than a male's pension fund. Considerations such as age differences between spouses are likely to impact upon pension needs, with a younger spouse having longer to save for their retirement, and potentially therefore reducing their need for pension provision as part of the settlement. Pensions are rather complex by nature as different funds have different rules, nuances, risks and potential for future income on retirement.

Where it is proportionate to the value of the pension funds in question, it is common for a pension actuary to be jointly instructed by spouses to consider the pension assets available to them, any complexities such as a complex fund structure, the fact a pension may already be in payment (i.e. one or both spouses are already retired and drawing their pension income), or distinctions being made of monies in pension funds accrued prior to the marriage or subsequent to the separation. The pension actuary then provides you both with a report containing their advice on how to achieve a fair settlement, and what percentage transfer should be made from one spouse to another, and logistically how that would work with your specific pension assets in mind.

It can be acceptable, where it is not proportionate to warrant the expense of an expert opinion, or if you are both far enough away from retirement, for you to simply agree that you will each keep your own pensions, or that a pension share should take place but you agree your own method of division, for example, a simple equalisation of the cash equivalent values. You can do a trade-off, which is referred to as 'offsetting', by saying one can, for example, receive a larger percentage of the house, in exchange for the other spouse retaining their pension. This is not an accurate method to share pension funds, but it can be used for ease and speed. These are broad-brush ways of dividing up your pension funds, even if they would not necessarily mean that you each have equal pension income on retirement.

If There's Money Left Over

Once needs have been met, and you have reasoned your fair division of your assets between you, you need to consider whether it is appropriate for any money left in excess of each of your needs to be fairly shared between you, and to do so you should consider 'compensation and sharing' as part of the Section 25 Factors. Compensation and sharing are rarely a deciding factor in most people's financial separation because it only applies to big-money cases where there is sufficient money to start with to meet each spouse's needs and thereafter further money left over.

It used to be that once needs were met, the remaining assets were retained by the person who legally owned them. This tended to be discriminatory as typically one spouse was the breadwinner and, once that breadwinner had met the other spouse's needs, they kept the rest which, as an overall proportion of the assets, would often tip the scales heavily in their favour. Nowadays the courts recognise the importance of other contributions spouses make to marriage. Being a homemaker is accepted as an equal contribution to the marriage and family life as being the breadwinner, and so case law has evolved to prevent a homemaker, for example, being discriminated against by their breadwinning spouse retaining a higher proportion of the assets to them.

It is from this school of thought that the considerations of fairness, compensation and sharing were established. Where there are excess monies beyond reasonable need, compensation is assessed. Should one spouse be compensated for any loss they may have suffered by virtue of their marriage? For example, did they give up a career with good potential as part of their marital decision that they should be a homemaker, raise their children, and support the other spouse's career and enable them to flourish? The general guidance is that the longer the marriage, the more reason there is for equal sharing of the overall assets. Equally sharing in each spouse's endeavours is more likely to be determined as fair in long marriage cases as marriage is viewed as a partnership, where each spouse's contributions, monetary or otherwise, should be equally rewarded.

Exceptions

There are some exceptions to these already rare big-money situations. The type of assets that remain after needs have been met are usually categorised and, depending on their categorisation, it might mean that they are exempt from the general rules of compensation and sharing. The financial positions of you and your spouse are often loosely referred to as 'the matrimonial pot' by family lawyers. There can then be arguments about 'ring-fencing' assets, meaning to keep them out of the matrimonial pot and not therefore available for division. To ring-fence an asset, it needs to fall into a set category, such as assets that were inherited and assets that are non-marital, meaning they were acquired before the marriage or post-separation.

For an asset to be ring-fenced because of it being in one of these special categories, it must not have been 'intermingled' with the marital assets; it must have been kept separate by being in that one spouse's sole name and not used to meet marital needs. For example, if one spouse inherits some money, the money is 'intermingled' if that spouse uses it to pay down the mortgage on their family home, or puts it in an account in their joint names, or in their spouse's sole name. The money can be argued for 'ring-fencing' if it was placed in an account in the sole name of the inheriting spouse, and never used to meet any of the family's expenses, for example money was not taken from it to meet school fees, pay for holidays or pay off credit cards. There needs to be a very clear distinction of an asset (which, remember, is surplus to needs) being kept solely in the name of the spouse seeking to ring-fence it.

These same ring-fencing and intermingling rules apply to assets that were accrued or acquired prior to the marriage or after separation. The length of the marriage, which can include any cohabitation before the wedding if it led seamlessly (meaning without a break-up in between) to the marriage, may make a big difference as to whether a significant asset is available for division as part of the fairness of your settlement. If you cohabited before your wedding it will be important for you to try to carefully remember exactly when you started living together so that any assets accrued during that period (if your cohabitation led seamlessly to marriage) can be included as having been accrued during the marriage.

The date for separation has the same importance. If the new divorce laws (see page 57) have not yet come in, be cautious about correctly recording the date of your separation between you and your spouse within the court proceedings, as you are required to state it on your divorce petition, which is usually submitted to the court long before you get to the point of disputing whether an asset was accrued post-separation. Further, if you and your spouse permanently separate you can continue to make transfers of assets between you within the same tax year as your date of separation at no gain or loss, meaning you will not have to pay capital gains tax. I note this as caution about balancing between giving a specific date of your separation to ring-fence assets acquired up to that time, against giving a date that allows you to make asset transfers between you, post-separation. It can be difficult to pinpoint an exact separation date, or even month, as there are two of you involved in the separation and it may not be clear when you jointly agreed that the separation had become permanent.

There are many arguments that spouses try to raise to break away from an equal division of the surplus assets. In a situation where one spouse has committed adultery the question is asked whether their morally bad behaviour should be reflected in the division of the assets – for example, whether they should be punished for being an adulterer by getting a lower proportion of the assets. The answer is no. Remember that needs come first and then, if there are surplus assets or income, only in certain situations can a person's behaviour be considered. A spouse's behaviour must be so exceptional and extreme that it would be unfair for it not to be taken into consideration, such as an attempt on the life of their spouse. Unacceptable financial behaviour might include a spouse spending gratuitous sums on gambling and losing the money in significant detriment to the matrimonial pot. It is rarely a successful argument to run so proceed only on the advice of a family lawyer.

A slightly different 'behavioural' issue that is more commonly raised in cases that have been disputed through the courts is a spouse's litigation misconduct. It is not uncommon for a spouse to try to avoid providing their full and frank financial disclosure, even when they have been ordered to do so by the court. Litigation misconduct can be punished by costs orders being made against them, so that they pay for the increased costs their spouse is having to incur because of their litigation misconduct. In serious cases, such as a spouse repeatedly failing to comply with court orders for disclosure of an asset or assets, a judge can punish them by imprisonment and/or fine them for being in contempt of court. You and your spouse have not only an initial duty to provide full and frank disclosure to each other, whether done voluntarily or as part of court proceedings, but also an ongoing duty to provide updated disclosure throughout the process and it is important that you engage in this process otherwise there is a risk of costs orders being made against you.

I should add that if you are in the big-money situation and there are surplus assets or income available for division after each of your needs are met, then you can, if it might apply to your circumstances, run as many of the above arguments for an unequal division as you like – you are not limited to just picking one. You should consider each surplus asset individually and categorise it independent of any other assets.

PERSONAL BELONGINGS, HOUSE CONTENTS AND PETS

While formal legal ownership matters less for married couples, I recommend reading page 212 for advice on how to divide your personal belongings, house contents and any pets between you. As I say, the formal legal ownership can be changed under matrimonial law, so just because an item, such as a car, is in the legal name of one spouse does not mean that it cannot be retained by the other (and formally transferred as part of the settlement, such as the V5 (vehicle logbook) being signed to transfer ownership over).

Costs

I have set out on page 250 the option for the applicant spouse to ask a court to make an order that the respondent spouse should pay some or all of their costs of the divorce. This is not to be confused with their costs of settling the financial issues, which are separate and distinct. The usual rule is that you each pay your own costs. However, it is still common for one spouse to hold most of the marital assets in their sole name, which means the other spouse does not have access to funds or have a big enough income of their own from which to meet their ongoing legal fees.

If you have concerns about funding your legal costs and you believe it is proportionate and reasonable for you to continue to have legal representation, you should try to agree with your spouse that they will transfer a lump sum to you to give you some provision. This is, of course, on the understanding that you believe your spouse has access to funds to make it affordable. If you cannot reach agreement, you can make an application to court for a 'legal services order', which forces your spouse to pay some or all of your legal fees. However, you are required to prove that you cannot source funding from lenders, such as a high street bank, credit card or specialist litigation loan company, first. You will need to make such applications formally to evidence your case that you cannot, independent of your spouse, raise funds to meet your legal costs, but that they can afford to assist you.

Litigation lenders can be very useful in this situation as they are able to provide funding bespoke to your financial case, which by this point will be a court dispute (you cannot make an application for your spouse to pay your legal fees without first having started court proceedings for a financial order, whether that be with legal representation or as a litigant in person if you have chosen or not been able to afford legal fees so far). They used to charge high rates of interest but tended to lend to spouses where more traditional lenders would not. I know that many litigation lenders have now reduced their rates and fees, but be aware that your family lawyer is usually required to be a part of the process and enter the loan contract with you. The contracts sometimes require your solicitor's law firm to agree that they will repay your loan if you default, and many law firms are not willing to form part of your litigation loan contract if it means their firm is exposed to your financial risk. You are obliged to check your eligibility for a litigation loan and there are enough out there that provide these services that you will likely find one which, if they agree to lend, would suit you and your family lawyer's terms.

If you are in a situation where you do need to make a court application for your spouse to pay, be aware that you must comply with certain procedural requirements and, if you fail to do so and you are unsuccessful in your application at court, you will be at risk of having a costs order made against you for your spouse's costs of dealing with that issue. You should take the advice of a family lawyer in either making such an application or if one is being made against you.

Remember that if you are the spouse being asked to provide a lump sum so that your spouse can afford to take legal advice, it is likely to be pragmatic and sensible for you to make such a provision. Firstly, it is not good for your amicability if you are adding to your dispute a further issue about funding legal fees, and you should consider whether it is proportionate for you to continue that argument or agree and save the costs. Secondly, if you refuse and your spouse does obtain a loan for their legal fees, the marital pot will suffer to the extent of any interest payable on that loan. If it is a litigation loan, the interest and fees accruing on that loan are likely to be significant. Thirdly, remember that their legal fees will have to be paid somehow, and will deplete the marital capital pot whether it is paid from your savings during the proceedings, or repaid from that same capital pot (potentially having also incurred interest and fees) once your settlement is finalised.

Obtaining a Court Order

However you reach a settlement between you, whether it is direct between you, with the use of a third party such as a friend, a professional such as a family lawyer, mediator or arbitrator, or if your dispute is argued through court, it is vital that your financial settlement is recorded in a court order to make it all legal and final.

If your final settlement is not formally recorded between you then your financial claims against each other as spouses will remain open, even if you finalise your divorce. This means that as you move forward with your lives you are not fully able to rely on the terms of the settlement you have reached, and may not be able to enforce that settlement against your ex-spouse if they later change their mind or fail to do something they had agreed to do by a set date. For example, if you agreed that your spouse will pay to you a lump sum of £20,000 by 5 January, but that date passes without receipt of the money, you have no immediate recourse to that money or power to enforce that transfer from your spouse without it being confirmed in an approved court order.

If you ask for a court order to be made in terms that you have agreed on yourselves it is called a 'consent order', meaning a court order made by the consent of the spouses. You can obtain a court order without having to go to court yourself. While you may have reached agreement based on who gets what, you will need a family lawyer to draft the consent order and think about the detail, any practicalities of how to make your settlement work and how it should be drafted to make it legally binding.

A family lawyer should not only turn your agreement into a formally drafted court order, they should also assist you in building in as much protection and clarity to the drafting to reduce the potential for future disputes between you. Future disputes are common when the original drafting is unclear and therefore open to interpretation, and years down the line it is difficult to prove your interpretation is the correct one.

Practical advice can also be given, such as thinking about whether any safeguards can be drafted into the agreement to protect what you have agreed. These are the types of practical considerations that a family lawyer's experience and training will bring to the drafting of your order. You could try to draft your own order and submit it to the court for approval without lawyers, but they are legal documents which require legal knowledge and terminology to draft correctly. If not drafted correctly there is a risk that a judge will refuse to approve the order, or if it is approved, there are problems relying on it or enforcing it in the future (which are unlikely to be foreseeable to a lay person drafting such a legal document).

Once your court order is drafted and the wording is agreed between you, you must submit it to the court which can be done by post, so you need not attend in person. With the draft consent order both spouses must complete a form called a 'Statement of Information for a Consent Order' on which you each summarise your pre-settlement financial positions, setting out your capital, liabilities, pension and net income, along with a confirmation from you both that the information is accurate and a truthful reflection. Even though you have reached a settlement about your finances yourselves, a judge is still being asked to approve the terms and they do so in reference to the snapshot of your respective financial positions set out in the Statement of Information. It is possible, although rare, for a judge to decline to approve the terms of a consent order if they do not think the settlement terms are fair. Usually a judge will consider and approve the terms of your consent order and the court will stamp the order (known as 'sealing it') to confirm that it has been made and can now be effected and enforced if the terms are breached (you will need decree absolute in your divorce proceedings).

The earliest point at which you can send a draft consent order to the court for a judge's approval is after the pronouncement of the decree nisi in the divorce proceedings (see page 50). It is not usually recommended that spouses apply for a decree nisi to be made absolute until a financial settlement is reached and the consent order has been approved by a judge. This is because if one spouse died during the financial negotiations and before a final settlement was achieved, the surviving spouse would be financially better off as a widow than as a divorcee. Don't worry if decree absolute is pronounced before your financial settlement is agreed; there are other provisions in the law which allow financial claims to be made against a deceased's estate for their dependents if sufficient provision is not made by their will or intestacy rules.

If you do not reach agreement between you and therefore can't obtain a court order by consent, then you will need a judge to decide how your finances should be divided. It is rare for financial cases to go all the way through court and get to the third stage of the process – the final hearing – where a judge needs to make the decision and impose a court order upon you both. Usually spouses are represented by lawyers at court who draft the order in accordance with the judge's given decision. This is a less attractive way of obtaining that vital court order, but it is the only other means of finalising and legalising all financial matters between you in the absence of you reaching agreement with your spouse.

Changing your mind

If you reach an agreement with your ex-partner between the two of you and you both have a mutual understanding that you should be held to that agreement, changing your mind should not be done lightly. I have spoken a great deal about the importance of trust, and the impact of changing your mind on part or all of your agreement will do damage to your trust and therefore your ongoing relationship. Be mindful of the significance of your change of position and make sure it is for the right reason, proportionate to the potential damage it might cause and whether it is even legally possible.

If you have reached agreement about how to settle your financial matters there is a stage after which you will be bound by those terms. If you have agreed your settlement terms in mediation or via solicitors then those terms will have been put in writing and you will have both confirmed your agreement. Once you get to this stage of the agreement, even though those terms are not yet set out in a formal court order, they are likely to be considered as contractually binding upon you both which means they are likely to be upheld by a judge and enforceable against you if you tried to change your mind.

If you have reached agreement without legal advice or professional assistance (such as from a mediator), in my experience there is more scope for you to be able to subsequently change your mind. However, it would need to be for a good and valid reason that you could seek to alter the terms of your agreement.

Once your agreement has been turned into a court order the terms are binding upon you and will be enforceable. The settlement terms as to capital (such as housing, lump sums or shares) and pensions are once and for all and you will not be able to go back to court to change your mind, unless rare and unusual circumstances apply or the basis upon which you reached that agreement was a false representation, and knowing that information could have significantly changed the settlement.

To have a court approved order means you can both move forward with your separate lives knowing exactly where you stand financially. You will have made compromises along the way to get there, and it is very rare for one or both ex-spouses to feel like they've got exactly what they want or need. Nonetheless, you have an answer to one of the biggest concerns which has no doubt been worrying you. For the majority who waited, don't forget to now apply for your divorce to be finalised and apply for your decree absolute.

PART VI

THE FUTURE

CHAPTER 14

Practical Advice for Your Future

Y OUR FUTURE MAY include another significant relationship and so it is worth understanding how any future
relationships may affect your financial settlement from
your divorce, and/or think about what you can do during that
next relationship to avoid or limit any future breakdown issues
should they arise with your new partner.

Cohabitation and Remarriage

I have previously mentioned that spousal maintenance (not to
be confused with child maintenance, which is not affected
by cohabitation or remarriage) is variable upwards or downwards at any point during the term of its payment. If the
receiving spouse remarries, the maintenance payments will
stop. The paying spouse can simply stop making the payments
without needing a further court order.

If the receiving spouse starts a new relationship it can be
difficult to determine at what point that relationship moves to
'cohabitation', and it is the differing interpretations of this
which are a common cause of conflict between ex-partners.
The law suggests that cohabitation is an unmarried couple
living together and sharing their lives as 'husband and wife'.

To suggest that a couple are cohabiting because a new partner might stay overnight a few times a week is unlikely to reach this threshold, but many ex-partners find it frustrating paying spousal maintenance when someone else in staying with their ex-spouse. It can be difficult to prove the level of cohabitation, but I do not recommend spying on your ex-spouse to gather your own evidence. It will not reflect well on you and is probably easy to undermine as evidence.

Many try to pre-empt this dispute as part of their original financial agreement, and provision is often included in the agreement or court order that if the receiving spouse starts to live with another person, the spousal maintenance payments should either reduce or stop entirely. Cohabitation does not have an automatic effect on the payments of spousal maintenance. The reason is because, in law, cohabitees do not have financial responsibilities to each other and so if that new cohabiting relationship broke down, the receiving spouse might be left in a position of financial vulnerability if their maintenance has stopped and their new partner is not there to share their living expenses. If you get to this stage, you will need to discuss the downward variation or cessation of spousal maintenance and seek your ex-spouse's agreement. In the absence of agreement an application to court can be made. It will be advisable for both of you to take independent legal advice before the costs of court proceedings are unnecessarily incurred.

Preventative financial steps

If you move on and have a stable relationship with a new partner, you should consider whether you would benefit from taking preventative financial action once your relationship becomes permanent, to avoid a messy break-up should your relationship break down in the future. For unmarried couples, you should consider entering into a cohabitation agreement together, which can state:

- how you own assets, expressly separating out different types of assets held now or which might come in during your relationship
- who pays for what during your relationship
- what the financial arrangements will be if you have children together (now or in the future)
- what will happen financially should you break up

If you are engaged you can do the same in a prenuptial agreement, or if you have already gone on to marry, you can jointly enter into a postnuptial agreement.

You should find that you're much more generous to each other making these arrangements when you are happy in your relationship than when it is done post-break-up. These preventative agreements act like contracts between you and, as long as they have been properly entered into and are fair, they are likely to be upheld on a later separation. You will each need a family lawyer to advise you and draft the document for you. These agreements are particularly popular for those who have received, or expect to receive, an inheritance and want to protect that inheritance, or if there is a financial inequality between you that makes it proportionate to enter into such an agreement.

Writing a New Will

If you have an existing will that names your ex-partner in it, you should consider whether your wishes remain the same or whether you would prefer to alter your previous provision for them in the event of your death. If you are obtaining a divorce it will affect your will automatically by effectively removing your ex-spouse from it.

If you are in protracted divorce proceedings and die during that process, your spouse would still inherit under the terms of your will or under intestacy rules, as your spouse. If you decide that you want to change your will I recommend changing it sooner rather than later. Be mindful that, as spouses, you have financial responsibilities to each other and, if your spouse or children are financially dependent upon you, you should take advice from a specialist wills lawyer to determine what provision you should make for your dependents in your will to prevent your ex-spouse being able to challenge it after your death.

Positive Communication

Whatever your issue or reason for your separation, try not to engage in negative communications with your ex-partner, though I appreciate that this is easier said than done and may not come naturally in your situation depending on what has gone on between you. I always tell my clients not to put themselves in the line of fire when communicating with their ex-partner. If you know that what you want to say is likely to cause a negative response, think about whether you need to say anything at all. If you still feel the point needs to be made, think about the best way to communicate it.

Talking in a public location, such as a café or restaurant, holds you both more accountable for your behaviour because you are in public view. It removes you from emotive locations, such as your shared home or former shared home, and allows either of you to remove yourself from the situation should it be necessary. It is advisable to avoid alcohol consumption if you do choose this option. Talking together in a public location places you both firmly at the centre of resolving your issues and gives a purpose to the discussions if you both understand the topics to be discussed in advance. You can then pre-think ahead of that meeting what it is you want to say and how you would like to say it.

If talking on the phone or face-to-face leads to arguments, try switching to written communications and keeping it to business hours only. Once you have found an improved method of communication, try to focus on the necessity of the message, the tone being used and the purpose. It will not help you to engage in negativity, although that is not to be confused with compromise. If changing your approach to your ex-partner does not work then try a non-court resolution option next (see Chapter 5).

Focus On Your Children

It seems obvious to say this, and I'm sure you would say that you do, however, it is very easy to let emotions get the better of you and be pulled into negative conversations, or arguments, about who did what to upset the other. By giving yourself the focus and boundary of making everything about your children, you will have more discipline about which discussions you engage in, and rightly place your children at the forefront and centre of your ongoing relationship with your ex-partner.

When acting for clients I am their reminder of this, and help them to focus on their children and make decisions about their best interests. I am their filter and their mouthpiece so we can work closely together to decide what needs to be communicated and how. I tell my clients, and sometimes the ex-partner too, that they need to be able to maintain that focus themselves and find a way to communicate, focused on their children, without lawyers as a crutch. Once your dispute is resolved the lawyers (or mediator or other third party you might have used) are no longer needed and will not be there going forward to assist in your ongoing communications.

I appreciate that it takes two to make co-parenting work and very often I have clients tell me that they are trying but their ex-partner is making things difficult or behaving in such a way that this approach is simply not realistic for them. Co-parenting requires effort, compromise and communication from both sides. All you can do is control what is within your control and that means maintaining your positivity, reasonableness and staying focused on your children.

My hope is that having read this book you will feel empowered to make progress with your ex-partner with more confidence in your viewpoint, knowing you are being reasonable and focusing on what's important. Separating physically, financially and emotionally, and potentially having an ongoing co-parenting relationship, is not easy, but you now have some tools to get through the issues and know when to ask for help.

Glossary of Legal Terms

Barrister or counsel

Can also generically be referred to as a lawyer. A barrister is instructed by a solicitor to work as part of a team with the solicitor and the client. Their day-to-day job is to represent clients in court and present their cases to the judges. They are also used to give second opinions. Some barristers are now able to be instructed direct by the client where the client is representing themselves in court proceedings without a solicitor. This option is referred to as 'direct access'.

CAFCASS

The Children and Family Court Advisory and Support Service, which is involved in every children's case by the court to assist with assessing what is in the child's best interest.

Capital needs

Your estimated capital requirements, which are your capital expenditure, housing, car, home improvements, retraining, etc.

Child arrangements order

A court order determining with whom a child should live and spend time with its parents (and sometimes other significant people in their life). This can also be obtained by consent, and be a child arrangements order by consent of the parties, also referred to as a 'consent order'.

Cohabitee/cohabiting

When two unmarried people are in a relationship together and live together like a married couple.

Consent order

A court order in which the terms set out in the order have been decided by the ex-partners themselves. They can be used in all types of family law matters to include children's disputes and financial separation.

Financial remedy proceedings

When a spouse makes a court application for a financial order alongside their divorce proceedings, the financial proceedings are referred to as 'financial remedy proceedings'. An order made by a judge as part of these proceedings is a 'financial remedy order'. One made by the consent of the parties will be a 'financial remedy order by consent' or a 'consent order'.

Former matrimonial home

The last home in which you lived as husband and wife. It is often abbreviated to 'FMH'.

Income needs

Your estimated itemised annual expenditure for you and, if applicable, your children.

Litigant in person

Someone who is representing themselves in court proceedings without a solicitor or barrister acting on their behalf.

Maintenance

Money from one ex-partner's income transferred to the other ex-partner paid either for the benefit of their children (child maintenance) or spouse (spousal maintenance). Spousal maintenance is not available to unmarried ex-partners – they will only have claims for child maintenance.

McKenzie friend

A person asked to assist a litigant in person. Usually it is by attending a court hearing with them, taking notes and talking to them (but not talking on their behalf to the judge or the other party in the proceedings).

Non-court dispute resolution

Alternative methods to resolving your dispute with the aim of avoiding court.

Non-molestation order

A court order preventing a person (usually an ex-partner or other closely connected person) from causing another person harm or threatening harm. Restrictions are placed on the person and and it is a criminal offence to breach any of the conditions imposed on them by the non-molestation order.

Occupation order

A court order preventing a person otherwise entitled to occupy a property, usually the family home, from continuing to live there for a specific period of time.

Parental responsibility

A right and responsibility to engage in and be consulted about significant decisions for a child such as their health, education, religion, whereabouts and name.

Pension sharing order

One spouse receives a transfer of a set figure or percentage of their spouse's pension fund into a pension fund in their own name.

Prohibited steps order

A court order available in children's proceedings which stops, usually, a parent from a parental responsibility decision, such as preventing them from moving their child to a new school, moving their child to a new location or taking their child abroad.

Solicitor

As a generic term, a solicitor can also be referred to as a lawyer. In England and Wales the legal profession which represents clients is split between solicitors and barristers. Solicitors are those who are first instructed to advise and progress a client's case on a day-to-day basis, communicating with the client, the ex-partner or their representatives, any third parties and the court on their client's behalf.

Specific issue order

A court order available in children's proceedings to decide a dispute about a child between, usually, its parents in relation to a parental responsibility decision. Those 'specific issues' can include the location of where a child should live (but not with whom the child should live and when, that is a child arrangements order), whether they can be taken on holiday, move location, change schools, change their name or have medical treatment.

Resources

British Association for Counselling and Psychotherapy

https://www.bacp.co.uk

Child abduction

www.gov.uk/government/publications/international-parental-child-abduction/international-parental-child-abduction

Children and Family Court Advisory and Support Service (CAFCASS)

http://cafcass.gov.uk

Divorce

www.gov.uk/divorce

Domestic abuse

https://www.gov.uk/guidance/domestic-abuse-how-to-get-help

Institute of Family Law Arbitrators

http://ifla.org.uk

Land Registry

https://www.gov.uk/government/organisations/land-registry

Legal Resources

Lexis Nexis and Practical Law have been legal resources used by the author in writing this book.

Legislation

- The Children Act 1989
  https://www.legislation.gov.uk/ukpga/1989/41/contents
- The Civil Partnership Act 2004
  http://www.legislation.gov.uk/ukpga/2004/33/contents
- The Matrimonial Causes Act 1973
  https://www.legislation.gov.uk/ukpga/1973/18

Relate

www.relate.org.uk

Resolution First for Family Law

http://resolution.org.uk

INDEX